The Palestinians and the Disputed Territories

**Other books in the
World's Hot Spots series:**

Afghanistan
Iraq
North Korea
Pakistan
Saudi Arabia

THE WORLD'S H🔥T SPOTS

The Palestinians and the Disputed Territories

Neil Alger, *Book Editor*

Daniel Leone, *President*
Bonnie Szumski, *Publisher*
Scott Barbour, *Managing Editor*

GREENHAVEN PRESS ®

THOMSON
GALE

San Diego • Detroit • New York • San Francisco • Cleveland
New Haven, Conn. • Waterville, Maine • London • Munich

THOMSON

✳ ™

GALE

Cover credit: AP/Wide World Photos

LIBRARY OF CONGRESS CATALOGING-IN-PUBLICATION DATA
The Palestinians and disputed territories / Neil Alger, book editor.
p. cm. — (The world's hot spots)
Includes bibliographical references and index.
ISBN 0-7377-1490-5 (pbk. : alk. paper) — ISBN 0-7377-1489-1 (lib. : alk. paper)
1. Arab-Israeli conflict. I. Alger, Neil. II. Series.
DS119.7.P288354 2004
956.04—dc21   2003048327

Printed in the United States of America

🔥 CONTENTS

Chapter 1: A Land Divided

1. The Origins of the Israeli-Palestinian Conflict
Although it is possible to trace the roots of the Israeli-
Palestinian conflict all the way back to biblical times,
many scholars argue that the conflict in its current form
began to take shape at the turn of the twentieth century
with the start of Zionism and the international persecution of the Jews.

2. Israel and Palestine from World War II Through Camp David I
After World War II the international community wanted
to create a safe place for the Jews of the world to live
free of repression and anti-Semitism. However, over the
next quarter of a century, Israel and the surrounding region experienced serious turmoil and a number of military engagements.

3. The Palestinian Resistance Movement and the First *Intifada*
After Israel's war of independence in 1948–1949, a
number of large refugee camps were established just
outside the newly expanded borders of Israel for the
Arabs who had been displaced during the fighting. From
these camps emerged an important sense of Palestinian
national identity that made the first popular Palestinian
uprising, or *Intifada*, possible.

Chapter 3: The Paths to Peace

T he American Heritage Dictionary defines the term *hot spot* as "an area in which there is dangerous unrest or hostile action." Though it is probably true that almost any conceivable "area" contains potentially "dangerous unrest or hostile action," there are certain countries in the world especially susceptible to conflict that threatens the lives of noncombatants on a regular basis. After the events of September 11, 2001, the consequences of this particular kind of conflict and the importance of the countries, regions, or groups that produce it are even more relevant for all concerned public policy makers, citizens, and students. Perhaps now more than ever, the violence and instability that engulfs the world's hot spots truly has a global reach and demands the attention of the entire international community.

The scope of problems caused by regional conflicts is evident in the extent to which international policy makers have begun to assert themselves in efforts to reduce the tension and violence that threatens innocent lives around the globe. The U.S. Congress, for example, recently addressed the issue of economic stability in Pakistan by considering a trading bill to encourage growth in the Pakistani textile industry. The efforts of some congresspeople to improve the economic conditions in Pakistan through trade with the United States was more than an effort to address a potential economic cause of the instability engulfing Pakistani society. It was also an acknowledgment that domestic issues in Pakistan are connected to domestic political issues in the United States. Without a concerted effort by policy makers in the United States, or any other country for that matter, it is quite possible that the violence and instability that shatters the lives of Pakistanis will not only continue, but will also worsen and threaten the stability and prosperity of other regions.

Recent international efforts to reach a peaceful settlement of the Israeli-Palestinian conflict also demonstrate how peace and stability in the Middle East is not just a regional issue. The toll on Palestinian and Israeli lives is easy to see through the suicide bombings and rocket attacks in Israeli cities and in the occupied territories of the West Bank and Gaza. What is, perhaps, not as evident is the extent to which this conflict involves the rest of the world. Saudi Arabia and Iran, for instance, have long been at odds and have attempted to gain control of the conflict by supporting competing organizations dedicated to a

Palestinian state. These groups have often used Saudi and Iranian financial and political support to carry out violent attacks against Israeli civilians and military installations. Of course, the issue goes far beyond a struggle between two regional powers to gain control of the region's most visible issue. Many analysts and leaders have also argued that the West's military and political support of Israel is one of the leading factors that motivated al-Qaeda's September 11 attacks on New York and Washington, D.C. In many ways, this regional conflict is an international affair that will require international solutions.

The World's Hot Spots series is intended to meet the demand for information and discussion among young adults and students who would like to better understand the areas embroiled in conflicts that contribute to catastrophic events like those of September 11. Each volume of The World's Hot Spots is an anthology of primary and secondary documents that provides historical background to the conflict, or conflicts, under examination. The books also provide students with a wide range of opinions from world leaders, activists, and professional writers concerning the root causes and potential solutions to the problems facing the countries covered in this series. In addition, extensive research tools such as an annotated table of contents, bibliography, and glossaries of terms and important figures provide readers a foundation from which they can build their knowledge of some of the world's most pressing issues. The information and opinions presented in The World's Hot Spots series will give students some of the tools they will need to become active participants in the ongoing dialogue concerning the globe's most volatile regions.

⬥ INTRODUCTION

Israel and Palestine: A Hundred Years of Conflict

On September 28, 2000, Ariel Sharon, chairman of the right-wing Israeli Likud Party, led a group of soldiers from the Israeli Defense Forces (IDF) to the al-Haram al-Sharif, also known as the Temple Mount, and provided the match that relit the fire of violence between Israelis and Palestinians. At the time, the atmosphere throughout the Middle East was one of charged tension mixed with the disappointment generated by the failure of the Oslo final status negotiations at Camp David the previous July. Whereas the Israelis placed the blame for the disintegration of the talks on Palestinian president Yasser Arafat, the Palestinians blamed the Israelis.

It was in the middle of this uncertain moment that Ariel Sharon announced his desire to visit the al-Haram al-Sharif, the third holiest site for practitioners of Islam. Ownership of the contested site was split between the Israelis and the Palestinians, with Israel in control of the Western, or Wailing, Wall, and the Palestinians in control of the area above, including the al-Aqsa mosque and the Dome of the Rock. Because of its importance to both Jews and Muslims, the Temple Mount area has played a major role in the politics of the region, with neither side willing to cede control. In fact, sovereignty over the al-Haram al-Sharif had been one of the breaking points in the failed Camp David talks.

Given the dangerous political environment at the end of September 2000, Ariel Sharon was counseled against making the trip because Palestinians would likely see the visit as antagonistic. Against the judgment of prominent Israeli and Palestinian leaders, Sharon chose to escort the troops through the Temple Mount, and the Al-Aqsa *Intifada* (second *Intifada*) was born.

There are different hypotheses regarding Ariel Sharon's motivations for making such a provocative gesture during such a politically tense moment. Some people believe that he wanted to win support within the Likud Party to edge out his rival, Benjamin Netanyahu. Others believe that Sharon's goal was indeed to incite a violent response from the Palestinians in order to further certain political goals. However, although it is convenient to point to his controversial visit to the al-Haram al-Sharif as the catalyst for this violent and confusing period, in order to truly understand the dimensions of the second *Intifada*, it is necessary to look deeper and understand the roots of the conflict as a whole. The Israel-Palestine conflict has been active for the last hundred years, and although the face of the hostilities has changed over time, many of the fundamental issues are still far from being resolved.

The History of Conflict

At the most fundamental level of the conflict, the fighting between Israelis and Palestinians is a dispute over landownership. During the nineteenth century and up through the end of World War I, Palestine was part of the vast Ottoman Empire consisting primarily of Arab Muslims but also small percentages of Christians and Jews. At the end of World War I, control of Palestine passed to the British, who made contrary promises to three groups who wanted sovereignty over the region: the Zionist Jews, the Arabs already living in Palestine, and the French. It is here that the political ambiguities over ownership of the land are often considered to have begun. On July 24, 1922, the British received an official mandate to operate as the controlling body of the region of Palestine, and almost immediately there was conflict between the British, the Jews, and the Arabs who shared the land. These conflicts escalated, along with the size of the Jewish population in Palestine, as more Jews emigrated from areas where anti-Semitism was threatening to explode.

In 1936 these conflicts reached a breaking point, and an Arab uprising surged for three years against both the British control over the Arab populations and the rising number of Jewish immigrants. At the end of the violent encounter, the British issued the MacDonald White Paper, or policy paper, that limited the total Jewish immigration to Palestine to seventy-five thousand over the next five years, at which time all further immigration would cease, unless the Arabs of Palestine agreed to allow more. And although the League of Nations declared the MacDonald White Paper illegal, the British attempted to continue to enforce the policy, even as the situation in many parts of the world became more precarious for the Jewish Diaspora through World War II.

After World War II, amid rising tensions between all three groups, the British announced that they would pull out of Palestine by August 1948, ceding control to the recently formed United Nations. On November 29, 1947, the United Nations issued UN General Assembly Resolution 181, which called for the splitting of Palestine into two states, one Jewish and one Arab, once the British had officially retreated from power. The Arab population in Palestine, which felt that its historical presence as the ethnic majority in the region should entitle it to more than half the territory, did not accept this resolution. Again, violent conflict between the Jews and Arabs flared in Palestine.

Amid this violence, on May 15, 1948, the state of Israel declared its independence. What followed was a war between Israel and the surrounding Arab nations. Even though the members of the UN Security Council had stated in UN General Assembly Resolution 181 that they "determine as a threat to the peace, breach of the peace or act of aggression . . . any attempt to alter by force the settlement envisaged by this resolution,"[1] when the war finally ended, the results were disastrous for the Arab Palestinians; Israel now controlled not just the 56 percent of mandate Palestine that had been allotted it by UN Resolution 181 but also another 21 percent that had been captured during the war. Further, more than seven hundred thousand Arabs had fled from the territories occupied during the campaign, and the Palestinian refugee problem was born. More than half a century later, these people have still been unable to return to their homes, even though international law states that all territories taken during military activity must be returned when the fighting is over.

Since the Israel War of Independence, the region has been devastated by a handful of further military clashes. In 1967, during the Six-Day War, Israel took control of the remainder of mandate Palestine as well as the Golan Heights from Syria and the Sinai Peninsula from Egypt. Israel then went to war with Egypt again in 1969 and 1973, invaded Lebanon in 1978, and fought directly with Palestinians during the popular Palestinian uprising in 1987 known as the first *Intifada*. Throughout this violent history, the United Nations has continually called for Israelis and Arabs to cease fire and for Israel to return to its borders as stipulated in 1947 in UN Resolution 181.

The Second *Intifada*

Since September 2000 violence has been a constant in the lives of Israelis and Palestinians alike. According to many Palestinians, the second *Intifada* erupted as a result of a series of frustrations among the Palestinian people. Since the state of Israel declared its independence from the British on May 15, 1948, the dream of a legitimate Palestinian state has remained just that. Huge population increases in Palestinian cities and refugee camps, combined with high levels of unemployment and constant oversight by the IDF, have created a situation where a large percentage of the Palestinian population is made up of young people who resent the conditions in which they feel they are being forced to live. For some of these young Palestinians, violence in the form of terrorism seems to be the only possible way to fight back against the Israelis, who maintain a tremendous military advantage over most of the Middle East.

The second *Intifada* has been characterized by a cycle of violence, where one attack prompts a retaliation, which in turn prompts another attack, and so on. For example, a suicide bombing attack by a Palestinian extremist group in Jerusalem might trigger an incursion by the IDF into a Palestinian refugee camp to crack down on known members of violent groups. These IDF raids often result in relatively high numbers of civilian casualties, which then prompt another suicide bombing in retaliation. In this way, the violence builds on itself, punctuated by occasional moments of quiet.

Another defining characteristic of the second *Intifada* is the high number of casualties suffered by civilians. From September 9, 2000, to May 14, 2003, 2,107 Palestinian noncombatants were killed and 5,933 were wounded by the "Israeli occupation forces and settlers"[2] in the occupied territories, according the Palestinian Center for Human Rights. On the Israeli side, according to the IDF, from September 9, 2000, through June 6, 2003, there were 17,763 terrorist incidents, causing 781 Israeli deaths, and 5,481 injuries. Furthermore, 3,851 of those injured and 545 of those who were killed were Israeli civilians. Given these statistics, it is apparent that the Israeli-Palestinian conflict has become increasingly dangerous for civilians since the uprising began in September 2000.

The Move to Violence

Many of the militant Palestinian extremist groups, such as Hamas and Islamic Jihad, are based on a fundamentalist Muslim ideology that calls for its followers to take up jihad, or holy war, in the struggle to control the holy land. These groups believe that they have a religious right to the land "from the river to the sea," or of all of Palestine from the Jordan River to the Mediterranean Sea, and are prepared to use any means necessary to achieve a united Islamic Palestine. Many of these groups have ties to the political side of the Palestinian struggle for statehood, such as the relationship between Hamas and the leading political party, Fatah, but opt for violent attacks in their attempts to catalyze change in the region.

Violence from the Israeli side tends to come from the IDF, which is charged with the task of keeping Israel's citizens safe from outside attack. In an attempt to guarantee the well-being of all Israelis, over the course of the second *Intifada*, the IDF has frequently occupied major Palestinian population centers, including Ramallah, where Palestinian president Yasser Arafat maintains his headquarters. These occupations usually employ curfews and strict regulations, which are often enforced by violent means. During these occupations, civilian casualty rates can be high, and when combined with the practice of demolishing homes and tearing apart Palestinian infrastructure (such as schools, businesses, utilities, etc.), repeatedly provoke serious reprisals from both the Palestinians and the international community at large.

The Settlement Issue

At the heart of the Israel-Palestine conflict is the issue of Israel's continued occupation of lands that were initially to be granted to the Palestinian people by the United Nations in 1947. According to international law, all territory that is occupied during military conflict must be returned when the conflict is ended. Under this rule, Israel should be required to return the land to the Palestinians. However, the Israelis make the argument that, because the occupied territories were never officially part of a sovereign nation since UN Resolution 181 was not actually implemented, Israel is only functioning as the administrator for the territory until a final status can be decided upon.

Another way in which Israel is in constant violation of international law is the institutionalized construction of settlements within the territories that Israel has occupied. Article 49 of the Fourth Geneva Convention states that "the Occupying Power shall not . . . transfer parts of its own civilian population into the territory it occupies,"[3] and yet every year more settlements are constructed. According to Peace Now, an Israel nongovernmental organization that watches and reports on settlement activities, in a report from September 5, 2002, the Israeli settler population in the West Bank has reached approximately 380,000 people, spread out over 145 official settlements and 105 unofficial settlements, or outposts. At the time of the report, somewhere between 220,000 and 250,000 of the West Bank settlers were concentrated in annexed East Jerusalem. And in the Gaza Strip, where 1 million Arabs live in one of the most densely populated areas in the world, 7,500 Jewish settlers control 30 percent of the territory. Furthermore, to maintain the safety of the settlers, secure access roads between the settlements and the major Israeli cities have cut the Palestinian-controlled areas into a series of separated islands. Trade between Palestinian cities has been hurt because access to neighboring areas has been cut off by large fenced-off spans and walls surrounding settlement areas. In effect, the Israeli settlements have isolated the Palestinian people from one another and made travel between cities a difficult task.

The Right of Return

As the Israeli settlement program pushes farther into Palestinian-controlled areas, and larger and larger population centers expand in the occupied territories, the possibility that Palestinian refugees will be allowed to return to their homes that they fled in the various wars diminishes rapidly The Palestinian right of return has been an important rallying point for Palestinian nationalist groups and a major sticking point in many of the attempted peace processes since the 1967 war.

But for the Israelis, the Palestinian right of return represents a major threat to the fundamental idea that generated the state of Israel, as stated early on in the Balfour Declaration of 1917: "The establishment in Palestine of a national home for the Jewish people."[4] Israel, as a functional democracy, is shaped by its citizens. If the Palestinian right of return is granted, the Jewish population will eventually become a minority to the Arab population. Many Israelis feel that this possible eventuality is reason enough to continue to go against international law and maintain control of the occupied territories while disallowing the Palestinian refugees to return to their old homes.

Jerusalem

Jerusalem houses major holy sites for Jews, Muslims, and Christians alike. For this reason, the international community sees a great importance in maintaining Jerusalem as an open city. In UN Resolution 181, while the rest of mandate Palestine was to be partitioned into two states, the city of Jerusalem was to become an international zone, which would operate independently of the Jewish and Palestinian states and be monitored by an international UN administration. However, both Palestinians and Israelis envision the city of Jerusalem as the capital of their own sovereign state.

The armistice agreement following the 1948 war split the city of Jerusalem in half, into East Jerusalem and West Jerusalem. Jordan annexed the eastern section, and the residents were given Jordanian citizenship in the 1950s. However, in the 1967 war Israeli forces occupied East Jerusalem and then annexed the territory in 1980. Because of its contested nature, and because it serves as a border between Israeli-controlled areas and Palestinian territory, Jerusalem has been the locus of much of the violence during the second *Intifada*. The greater metropolitan area of Jerusalem is dotted with IDF outposts and checkpoints on roads between Palestinian and Israeli sectors.

The Quartet Roadmap for Peace

In 1993, with the signing of the Declaration of Principles of the Oslo Peace Accords by Yasser Arafat and Israeli prime minister Yitzhak Rabin on the White House lawn, the Israeli-Palestinian peace process took on a new format. According to Mark Tessler, a historian of the conflict,

> Even though [the Declaration of Principles] left substantive issues unresolved, making a contribution that was essentially symbolic and emotional, the accord gave each party the recognition it had long sought from the other and confirmed before the world that there is nothing about the essence of either Zionism or Palestinian nationalism that makes a solution to the conflict impossible. The accord demonstrated that the obstacles to peace are not insurmountable, that the parties can reach an accommodation based on territorial compromise and mutual recognition if they possess the political will to do so. In this respect, it introduced a revolutionary and perhaps irreversible change into the relationship between Israel and the Palestinians.[5]

Since 1993 the peace process has followed this concept of "accommodation based on territorial compromise and mutual recognition," but without reaching any final negotiation.

Following in the footsteps of the Declaration of Principles on April 30, 2003, U.S. president George W. Bush, along with the other Quartet members (the United Nations, the European Union, and the Russian Federation), presented the Quartet Roadmap, which lays out a time line for producing a lasting peace between the Israelis and Palestinians. Similar to the Oslo Peace Accords that were overseen by U.S. president Bill Clinton in 1993, the Quartet Roadmap envisions a two-state solution, where a legitimate Palestinian state coexists within the borders of mandate Palestine with the Jewish state of Israel.

The Quartet Roadmap is set up in such a way that both sides will make concessions at the same time. As the Palestinian government cracks down on militant organizations such as Hamas and Islamic Jihad, the two groups responsible for the majority of terror attacks on Israeli citizens, the Israeli government will pull out of small parts of the occupied territories and dismantle certain strategic settlements. In the same way that the violence between the two sides has traditionally escalated as a result of reciprocation, the hope is that the peace process will escalate as both sides gain greater trust in each other.

Although the process seems simple on paper, the reality of brokering a lasting peace is much more daunting. For the Israelis, a number of questions have been raised regarding whether the Palestinian government will be able to control the militant organizations. There are links between Hamas and Yasser Arafat's Fatah Party, but it is unclear how much control anyone will be able to exert over the militant group. In the past, cease-fires negotiated with Hamas have tended to disintegrate at the first Israeli provocation.

One way the Israelis have tried to deal with the issue of Palestinian control of militant groups is by stipulating the appointment of a Palestinian prime minister who, instead of Palestinian president Yasser Arafat, would be responsible for the suppression of militant terrorists. Arafat and the Palestinian National Council appointed Mahmoud Abbas, better known as Abu Mazen, just hours before the Quartet Roadmap was officially presented to the Palestinians. Abbas, who believed that an end to the militarized struggle is the only way for Palestinians to move toward their own legitimate state, met with Hamas in May and early June 2003 and appeared to be making progress. However, on June 6, 2003, top Hamas officials announced that the organization had already pulled out of the cease-fire negotiations without a resolution, making the possibility of implementing the Quartet Roadmap much more difficult.

From the Palestinian perspective, there are some dangerous aspects to the Quartet Roadmap. First of all, the roadmap does not specifically stipulate how many settlements will be dismantled or how much of the occupied territory will be returned to Palestinian sovereignty. As the Palestinian areas currently exist, they are isolated from one another by access roads and checkpoints. In order for the Palestinians to be able to accept the end result of the roadmap, they need to be assured that the resultant Palestinian state is set up in such a way that all of its citizens have the ability to move freely within its borders.

But even if all of these fears can be set aside, there is still one final issue with the Quartet Roadmap. Like the Oslo Peace Accords, the roadmap calls for immediate concessions from both sides to help establish trusting relationships across the negotiating table. However, also like the Oslo accords, it leaves two of the most important questions to the very end: the Palestinian right of return and the ultimate decision on the control of East and West Jerusalem. During the Oslo period, from 1993 to 2000, the inability to complete final status negotiations for these big questions derailed the possibility of a lasting peace agreement.

For militant Palestinian groups like Hamas, the Palestinian right of return is one of the foundational goals that these groups have been working toward since their inception. One reason that it is difficult for the Palestinian leadership to negotiate a cease-fire with Hamas is because the militant organization fears that the Palestinian right of return will go unfulfilled in the final agreement between the Israelis and the Palestinians.

As far as Jerusalem is concerned, both sides have been extremely reluctant to negotiate any sort of shared sovereignty of the holy city in the past. During the Oslo and Camp David talks of 1993 and 2000, President Bill Clinton offered a number of creative solutions to work out shared ownership of important holy sites and areas of the city but was still unable to convince either side to compromise their desire for full control.

By leaving key components until the final stages of the peace process, it is possible that the Quartet Roadmap, even though it produced significant cooperation in its earliest stage, may meet the same fate as the Oslo Peace Accords. Indeed, in the months following the initial agreement, violence between the Israelies and Palestinians continued. In September 2003, Abbas resigned as the Palestinian prime minster after a disagreement with Arafat, leaving the peace process further in doubt.

The conflict between Israelis and Palestinians has been nearly constant for the last hundred years and has taken up a place in the everyday lives of the citizens on both sides of their shared border. Fighting has spilled out into every neighboring Arab country at some point in the last fifty years, and the stability of the greater Middle East may well hinge on the possibility of a lasting peace treaty between these two warring peoples.

Notes

1. Quoted in United Nations website. www.UN.org.
2. Palestinian Center for Human Rights, *Killings and Injuries.* www.pchr.org.
3. Quoted in the International Committee of the Red Cross, full text of the Geneva Conventions. www.icrc.org.
4. Mark Tessler, *A History of the Israeli-Palestinian Conflict.* Bloomington: Indiana University Press, 1994, p. 148.
5. Tessler, *A History of the Israeli-Palestinian Conflict,* p. 756.

CHAPTER 1

A Land Divided

The Origins of the Israeli-Palestinian Conflict

By David Schafer

The story of Sarai and Abram from the book of Genesis in the Old Testament *is sometimes pointed to as the root of the conflict that currently rages between Israelis and Palestinians. Sarai, who was childless in her late seventies, counseled her husband Abram to have a child with her Egyptian handmaid, Hagar. Hagar bore a son named Ishmael. Thirteen years later, however, Sarai and Abram gave birth to a son, whom they named Isaac. As the story goes, Ishmael became the father of the northern Arabs, and Isaac the father of the Jews. Their rivalry as brothers is cited as the first instance of conflict between the Jews and the Arabs in the Holy Land.*

Although some of the ideologies that underscore the conflict can be traced back to biblical times, the conflict as it exists today is made up of a number of important factors that have come into play in much more recent years. These factors include the rise of international anti-Semitism, such as the violent pogroms in Russia during the nineteenth century. This article explores how the Zionist movement arose in reaction to this rampant anti-Semitism and sought a safe place to establish a country for the world's Jews. Eventually the Zionists settled on modern-day Israel as the ideal location.

This article also covers the contrary statements made by the British to both the Jews and the Arabs regarding who would live in Palestine after World War I, and it traces how those statements have led to two groups having claims to the same land. Written by David Schafer, this article originally appeared in the Humanist, *for which the author is a consulting editor.*

David Schafer, "Origins of the Israeli-Palestinian Conflict," *The Humanist*, vol. 62, July/August 2002, pp. 14–18.

W hen a problem gets so vast and so complex that it's hard to see how it can ever be resolved, it's perfectly natural to ask ourselves whether there was a time when, with sufficient foresight, it might have been prevented. If only we knew how to anticipate such problems, we tell ourselves, maybe we could avoid them in the future. So, applying that reasoning, let us ask how the seemingly intractable mess between the Palestinian people and the state of Israel ever got started?

The Religious Roots

We could blame it on Sarai, wife of Abram. According to the story in Genesis 16, it was Sarai's idea, when she was still childless in her late seventies, for Abram to have a child by her Egyptian handmaid, Hagar—so he did, and named the son Ishmael. But thirteen years later, according to Genesis 21, Sarai (now renamed Sarah) herself gave birth to a son by Abram (now Abraham), and this son was named Isaac. Sarah's actions led to rivalry between the descendants of Abraham's sons. According to traditions, Isaac became the progenitor of the Jews and Ishmael of the northern Arabs. Both sons were circumcised at God's command, but Hagar and her son were exiled to the southern desert. And exile is a major theme in both Hebrew and Arabic stories. *Hagar* is from the same Semitic root for emigrate as the Arabic *hijra*—the Hegira, Muhammad's emigration from Mecca to Medina in 622 CE, which is considered the starting point of Islam.

Or we could blame it on Pope Urban II, who in 1095 CE instigated the first Crusade. The next spring, according to Karen Armstrong in *Jerusalem:*

> A band of German Crusaders massacred the Jewish communities of Speyer, Worms, and Mainz upon the Rhine. This had certainly not been the pope's intention, but it seemed ridiculous to these Crusaders to march thousands of miles to fight Muslims—about whom they knew next to nothing—when the people who had actually killed Christ (or so the Crusaders believed) were alive and well on their very doorsteps. These were the first full-scale pogroms in Europe.

The word *pogrom* means "devastation" in Russian, and there were many pogroms in nineteenth-century Russia. When Ariel Sharon addressed soldiers of the Israeli Defense Force at Jenin in April 2002, he reminded them that their struggle had begun "120 years ago." This could only have referred to the pogrom that followed the assassination of Czar Alexander II in 1881, when one of the plotters was found to be a young Jewish woman. The first aliyah ("going up" to Israel) of Jews began the very next year with the arrival of fourteen European immigrants at Jaffa in Palestine. This was an insignificant number compared to the mainly Sephardic (Spanish-Mediterranean) Jews already in Palestine and Syria (around 25,000 in 1800), some of whose family roots had been there for a long time. However, the first aliyah continued until 1903 and was followed by many more.

The Start of Zionism

Or we might, if we choose, even blame the present troubles on Charles Darwin, whose promulgation of the idea of natural selection in the mid-nineteenth century was immediately picked up and twisted by "Social Darwinists" to support the notion that Aryans were inherently superior to the Semitic peoples and to justify anti-Semitic campaigns throughout Europe. It is important to remember, though, that whether such anti-Jewish discrimination took the form of pogroms or something less violent, it was carried out not by Palestinian Muslims but by European Christians. Those Jews who chose to emigrate to Palestine clearly saw it at the time as a better and safer place to be.

As far back as the 1860s a German Jew, Moses Hess, had advocated the formation of a Jewish "national home" in Palestine. At that time most Jews in western Europe did not take such an idea seriously. Many of them, emancipated by eighteenth-century Enlightenment ideas, had become successfully integrated into their societies and were comfortable where they were. By the 1880s, however, both western and eastern European Jews were beginning to be ready for this idea. Leo Pinsker advanced a proposal for a secular socialist Jewish state in his 1882 book *Auto-Emancipation.* Nathan Birnbaüm seems to have been the first to propose the term *Zionism* for this concept in 1886.

But the real impetus for the Zionist program came from a Viennese journalist, Theodor Herzl, who was shocked by the anti-Semitism demonstrated in the rigged trial and conviction for treason (in 1894 Enlightenment France, of all places) of Alfred Dreyfus, a Jewish officer. Herzl's 1896 book *Der Judenstaat* proposed that Jews should have their own nation-state. A superlative communicator, Herzl was able to bring the basic concept of Zionism to the attention of the world. The following year, on August 29, the first Zionist Congress met in Basel with the objective "to create for the Jewish people a home in Palestine secured by public law" and to promote the settlement of Palestine by skilled and professional Jews. Herzl himself was not personally committed to locating the new Jewish state in Palestine and seriously considered such places as the Sinai Peninsula, Kenya, and Cyprus.

Surprisingly, perhaps, there has been some resistance to Zionism from its very inception from the most orthodox elements in Judaism, based for the most part on three arguments: first, that Zionism is a secular movement and would imperil the essentially religious nature of

Judaism; second, that the indigenous Jews and Arabs of Palestine have enjoyed a harmonious relationship that would be disrupted by the introduction of European Zionists in large numbers; and last and most importantly, according to Jewish eschatology [the religious study of the end of mankind] a Jewish state must not be established until the Messiah comes to lead it. The proportion of Orthodox Jews who hold to these views is hotly debated; today they appear to be represented mainly by a branch known as Neturei Karta (an Aramaic name meaning "Guardians of the City").

The History of Hostilities

Nowadays, we have grown accustomed to hearing the present situation blamed not on Christian anti-Semitism but on intrinsic hostility between Muslims and Jews. Plenty of hostility has been built up on both sides over the past century, to be sure, but has it always been this way? Serious students, like Karen Armstrong in *Jerusalem*, William L. Cleveland in *A History of the Modern Middle East*, and I.J. Bickerton and C.L. Klausner in *A Concise History of the Arab-Israeli Conflict* are not quick to offer religious intolerance as a fundamental explanation of current events.

According to accounts of the early history of Islam, together with passages from the Quran and Hadith, Muhammad understood himself to be the last in a series of Jewish prophets, including Jesus, and his mission to be to renew the Jewish prophets' mission to Jews, Christians, and the whole world. The Quran uses the term *ahl al-kitab* (People of the Book) more than thirty times, mostly in Surahs 2–5, allotting special status to Jews and Christians as believers in the Torah and the Gospels (and later, when Islam spread to Persia, the term also included the Zoroastrians). Muhammad did reject those Jews who did not accept him as their prophet, and he regarded the Christian belief that Jesus was the son of God to be a form of polytheism. Still, as People of the Book, they were dhimmis (to be protected) under Muslim governments if they paid a jizya (poll tax).

In practice there was wide variation in the way Muslim authorities interpreted these rules, and instances are sometimes cited where Jews and Christians fared badly in areas ruled by Muslims. There are other cases, however, where Muslims, Jews, and Christians lived at peace together and even created a remarkably unified kind of community. Perhaps the most notable example is the Muslim city of Cordoba in Spain, where both the Jewish philosopher Moses ben Maimon (Maimonides) and the Arabic philosopher ibn Rushd (Averroes) were born and wrote in Arabic—described in the recent book *The Ornament of the World* by Maria Rosa Menocal.

The Growth of Palestine

The name Palestine originally meant "land of the Philistines." From Greek and Roman times, Palestine was often combined administratively with Syria to form Syro-Palestine. After the Ottoman conquest in 1516, most of Palestine was included in the vilayet (major administrative unit) of Syria. Much later, at the start of the nineteenth century, a weakened Ottoman Empire, having repeatedly failed to control Persia (now under the Qajar dynasty), was also forced to accept a semi-autonomous Egypt under Muhammad Ali. Among a series of expansionist moves east and south, Egypt captured Palestine west of the Jordan River—the part we now call "Palestine." Egypt held it from 1831 to 1840 before it returned to the Ottoman Empire, with the northern portion in the vilayet of Beirut and the southern in the smaller sanjak (district or "flag") of Jerusalem.

Between 1854 and 1869, Egypt built the Suez Canal. But in doing so it drove itself into bankruptcy and in 1882 became a British protectorate. Remember that around 1882 events in Russia and western Europe were leading toward the development of a Zionist movement and the start of Jewish immigration into Palestine. From 1882 on, proximity to the canal and to British power was to have a profound influence on Palestinian-Jewish relations.

The Yishuv, as the Jewish community in Palestine was called, began small and grew slowly during the years leading up to World War I. Immigration was funded mainly by a small number of wealthy European Jews, led by the French Baron Edmond de Rothschild, who was not a Zionist himself. Initially the land was owned by a few rich, mainly absentee landlords who lived in or near urban areas and occupied and worked by many poor peasant farmers (fellahin, in Arabic).

Usually the fellahin were driven off the land so that Jewish immigrants could occupy it. According to Justin McCarthy's *The Population of Palestine: Population, History, and Statistics of the Late Ottoman Period and the Mandate* (1990)—the definitive source for such population data—the first aliyah continued from 1882 to 1903, by which time about 90,000 acres were purchased, with about twenty villages and 10,000 new settlers, about half of them in the villages. Successive waves of immigrants varied strikingly in their past lifestyles, those from western or eastern Europe being more accustomed to urban or rural environments, respectively. Accordingly, some chose to work the land themselves while others hired back some of the fellahin. According to Bickerton and Klausner:

> Initial Arab peasant opposition subsided when the peasants realized that
> Jewish landowners would maintain the tradition of permitting them to

work the land and keep their income. The number of Jewish settlers was too small to have any serious impact upon Arab agriculture, especially in the hill country. Interestingly, public opposition to Zionist settlement was led by the Greek Orthodox Christians of Palestine.

Still other immigrants gave up and emigrated from Palestine. Of the 40,000 new immigrants arriving in the second aliyah, between 1904 and 1914 (David Ben-Gurion was one of the leaders of this group), some estimates say that as many as 90 percent found the conditions inhospitable and left. By 1914 there were still only about forty Jewish settlements in Palestine, owning about 100,000 acres. Of this land about 4 percent had been purchased by the Jewish National Fund (established in 1901), a protected source considered Jewish national property. In 1914 the total population of Palestine was about 722,000, of which only about 60,000 or 8 percent were Jews (12,000 in collective farms and villages). This would be a net increase of only 35,000 in 114 years. By contrast, during the same period, the number of Jews in Europe increased from two million to thirteen million. Equally striking is the fact that, while almost three million Jews left Russia between 1880 and 1914, only about 30,000 of them went to Palestine. After World War I, however, a radical change took place.

The British and Palestine

The British presence in India and the Far East depended increasingly on control of the Suez Canal and the Persian Gulf. When the Ottoman Empire joined Germany at the start of World War I in 1914, Britain seized the opportunity to strengthen its long-term position in the Middle East by courting support from Jews and especially Arabs, many of whom (though by no means all) had long chafed under Ottoman rule. Over the next three years, three separate policy statements emerged from these efforts, partially contradicting each other. Sir Henry McMahon, the British high commissioner in Egypt, sent a letter in Arabic to Hussain, Sharif of Mecca, on October 24, 1915, in effect offering independence to the Arabs who would support the British war effort.

The following June, under the leadership of Hussain's son Faisal, the Arab Revolt began. . . .

Meanwhile, the British government had been following different tacks in separate discussions with French and Zionist representatives about the postwar disposition of captured lands in the Middle East. In May 1916, the Sykes-Picot agreement gave France "influence" or outright control over the northern and western areas corresponding roughly to Syria, southeastern Turkey, and the upper Tigris-Euphrates valley of modern Iraq. The area corresponding most closely to modern Palestine would be governed by an "allied condominium." Then on November 2, 1917, Lord Arthur James Balfour, British foreign secretary, wrote to Lord Lionel Walter Rothschild, head of the British Zionist Organization, an influential "declaration" of two essential parts:

1. "His Majesty's Government view with favour the establishment in Palestine of a national home for the Jewish people, and will use their best endeavours to facilitate the achievement of this object."

2. "It being clearly understood that nothing shall be done which may prejudice the civil and religious rights of existing non-Jewish communities in Palestine, or the rights and political status enjoyed by Jews in any other country."

A Dangerous Contradiction

These two statements contained vague language and translation ambiguities that would later be interpreted as contradicting each other or the McMahon letter. It is of historical importance that Chaim Weizmann, a brilliant Russian chemist and charismatic Zionist leader who worked in London during the war and much later became Israel's first president, played a crucial role in persuading David Lloyd George, Winston Churchill, and others high in the British government to support the Balfour Declaration.

Misunderstandings became apparent as soon as the Paris peace conference began [in March 1919]. Looking for a way out, the British asked Faisal and Weizmann to negotiate personally in an effort to find common ground. Despite their own misgivings the two reached tentative agreement, only to find that everyone had underestimated the growing opposition of the local Arab population, now becoming fearful of Zionist expansion. As a result, the peace conference let the British and French settle Middle East divisions. The actual settlement resembled a simplified version of the Sykes-Picot Agreement, with "mandates" to be governed by Britain and France. The French mandate included modern Lebanon and Syria; the British mandate, modern Palestine, "Transjordan" (modern Jordan), and Iraq.

Neither Jews nor Arabs were happy with this outcome. Many Zionists were incensed by a ruling that Jewish immigration would not be permitted in Transjordan. This reaction led to the formation of a Jewish military group, which later became the terrorist organization Irgun. Much later outgrowths were the rise of Menachem Begin and the Likud party. Many Arabs likewise felt betrayed by the possibility of an eventual Jewish state within Palestine. With signs of violent resistance beginning to appear among both Jews and Arabs, the British government began to try to manage Jewish population growth by limiting or prohibiting Jewish immigration to Palestine through a series of three "White Papers" in 1922, 1930, and 1939. Winston Churchill, who was colonial secretary in 1922, issued the first of these. Each White Paper was enforced for a time but abandoned when opposition mounted to an unacceptable level.

Actual immigration reflected conditions in Europe with the approach and reality of World War II. Between 1914 and the start of the mandate and the end of the third aliyah (1922), there were 30,000 new immigrants. In the short space of the next fifteen years, the population of Palestine increased by almost 600,000. . . .

This alarmed the Arabs. William Cleveland comments in *A History of the Modern Middle East*, "It is little wonder that in a region of limited agricultural potential, the ownership of arable land became a matter of contention." He concludes:

> The cumulative effect of land transfers, British policy, and Arab notable attitudes was the increasing impoverishment and marginalization of the Palestinian Arab peasantry. Alienated from their own political elite, who seemed to profit from their plight; from the British, who appeared unwilling to prevent their expulsion from the land; and from the Zionists, who were perceived to be at the root of their problems, they expressed their discontent in outbreaks of violence against all three parties.

. . . Readers may wonder what this story has to do with today's Israeli/Palestinian conflict. As of the 1930s, the state of Israel had not come into existence, and the Palestinians were referred to merely as Arabs. The Holocaust had not yet occurred, nor had squalid Arab refugee camps developed. Yet as can easily be seen, all the troubles of the present situation are latent in the story told thus far.

Israel and Palestine from World War II Through Camp David I

By Joel Beinin and Lisa Hajjar

*In this article authors Joel Beinin and Lisa Hajjar trace the history of the Is-
raelis and Palestinians through the turbulent period following World War II
and up to the first major attempt at creating a lasting peace in the region, the
Camp David peace talks of 1978. The authors produced this report for the
Middle East Research and Information Project (MERIP), a nonreligious and
nonpartisan group working to provide nonbiased accounts of the conflicts in
the Middle East. MERIP also publishes* The Middle East Report. *Joel Beinin
is a professor of Middle Eastern history at Stanford University, and Lisa Hajjar is a professor of law and society at the University of California at Santa
Barbara.*

Following World War II, escalating hostilities between Arabs and
Jews over the fate of Palestine and between the Zionist militias and
the British army compelled Britain to relinquish its mandate over
Palestine. The British requested that the recently established United
Nations determine the future of Palestine. But the British government's
hope was that the UN would be unable to arrive at a workable solution, and would turn Palestine back to them as a UN trusteeship. A
UN-appointed committee of representatives from various countries
went to Palestine to investigate the situation. Although members of
this committee disagreed on the form that a political resolution should
take, there was general agreement that the country would have to be

divided in order to satisfy the needs and demands of both Jews and Palestinian Arabs. At the end of 1946, 1,269,000 Arabs and 608,000 Jews resided within the borders of Mandate Palestine. Jews had acquired by purchase 6 to 8 percent of the total land area of Palestine amounting to about 20 percent of the arable land.

On November 29, 1947, the UN General Assembly voted to partition Palestine into two states, one Jewish and the other Arab. The UN partition plan divided the country in such a way that each state would have a majority of its own population, although some Jewish settlements would fall within the proposed Palestinian state and many Palestinians would become part of the proposed Jewish state. The territory designated to the Jewish state would be slightly larger than the Palestinian state (56 percent and 43 percent of Palestine, respectively) on the assumption that increasing numbers of Jews would immigrate there. According to the UN partition plan, the area of Jerusalem and Bethlehem was to become an international zone.

Publicly, the Zionist leadership accepted the UN partition plan, although they hoped somehow to expand the borders allotted to the Jewish state. The Palestinian Arabs and the surrounding Arab states rejected the UN plan and regarded the General Assembly vote as an international betrayal. Some argued that the UN plan allotted too much territory to the Jews. Most Arabs regarded the proposed Jewish state as a settler colony and argued that it was only because the British had permitted extensive Zionist settlement in Palestine against the wishes of the Arab majority that the question of Jewish statehood was on the international agenda at all.

Violence Resumes

Fighting began between the Arab and Jewish residents of Palestine days after the adoption of the UN partition plan. The Arab military forces were poorly organized, trained and armed. In contrast, Zionist military forces, although numerically smaller, were well organized, trained and armed. By the spring of 1948, the Zionist forces had secured control over most of the territory allotted to the Jewish state in the UN plan.

On May 15, 1948, the British evacuated Palestine, and Zionist leaders proclaimed the state of Israel. Neighboring Arab states (Egypt, Syria, Jordan and Iraq) then invaded Israel claiming that they sought to "save" Palestine from the Zionists. In fact, the Arab rulers had territorial designs on Palestine and were no more anxious to see a Palestinian Arab state emerge than the Zionists. During May and June 1948, when the fighting was most intense, the outcome of this first Arab-Israeli War was in doubt. But after arms shipments from Czechoslovakia reached

Israel, its armed forces established superiority and conquered territories beyond the UN partition plan borders of the Jewish state.

In 1949, the war between Israel and the Arab states ended with the signing of armistice agreements. The country once known as Palestine was now divided into three parts, each under separate political control. The State of Israel encompassed over 77 percent of the territory. Jordan occupied East Jerusalem and the hill country of central Palestine (the West Bank). Egypt took control of the coastal plain around the city of Gaza (the Gaza Strip). The Palestinian Arab state envisioned by the UN partition plan was never established. . . .

After 1949, although there was an armistice between Israel and the Arab states, the conflict continued and the region remained imperiled by the prospect of another war. This was fueled by an escalating arms race as countries built up their military caches and prepared their forces (and their populations) for a future showdown. In 1956, Israel joined with Britain and France to attack Egypt, ostensibly to reverse

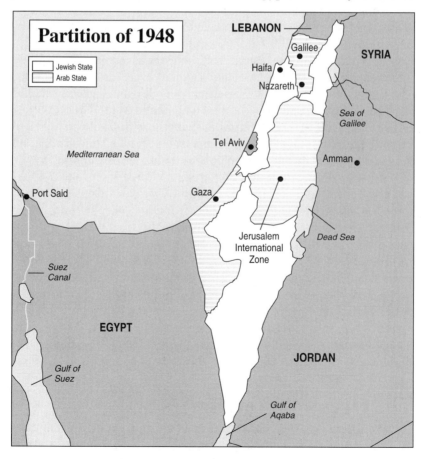

Partition of 1948

the Egyptian government's nationalization of the Suez Canal (then under French and British control). Israeli forces captured Gaza and the Sinai Peninsula, but were forced to evacuate back to the armistice lines as a result of UN pressure led by the US and the Soviet Union (in an uncharacteristic show of cooperation to avert further conflict in the Middle East). By the early 1960s, however, the region was becoming a hot spot of Cold War rivalry as the US and the Soviet Union were competing with one another for global power and influence.

The 1967 War

In the spring of 1967, the Soviet Union misinformed the Syrian government that Israeli forces were massing in northern Israel to attack Syria. There was no such Israeli mobilization. But clashes between Israel and Syria had been escalating for about a year, and Israeli leaders had publicly declared that it might be necessary to bring down the Syrian regime if it failed to end Palestinian commando attacks against Israel from Syrian territory.

Responding to a Syrian request for assistance, in May 1967 Egyptian troops entered the Sinai Peninsula bordering Israel. A few days later, Egyptian president Gamal Abdel-Nasser asked the UN observer forces stationed between Israel and Egypt to evacuate their positions. The Egyptians then occupied Sharm al-Shaykh at the southern tip of the Sinai Peninsula and proclaimed a blockade of the Israeli port of Eilat on the Gulf of Aqaba, arguing that access to Eilat was through Egyptian territorial waters. These measures shocked and frightened the Israeli public, which believed it was in danger of annihilation.

As the military and diplomatic crisis continued, on June 5, 1967 Israel preemptively attacked Egypt and Syria, destroying their air forces on the ground within a few hours. Jordan joined in the fighting belatedly, and consequently was attacked by Israel as well. The Egyptian, Syrian and Jordanian armies were decisively defeated, and Israel captured the West Bank from Jordan, the Gaza Strip and the Sinai Peninsula from Egypt, and the Golan Heights from Syria.

The 1967 war, which lasted only six days, established Israel as the dominant regional military power. The speed and thoroughness of Israel's victory discredited the Arab regimes. In contrast, the Palestinian national movement emerged as a major actor after 1967 in the form of the political and military groups that made up the Palestine Liberation Organization (PLO).

The Occupied Territories

The West Bank and the Gaza Strip became distinct geographical units as a result of the 1949 armistice that divided the new Jewish state of

Israel from other parts of Mandate Palestine. From 1948–67, the West Bank, including East Jerusalem, was ruled by Jordan, which annexed the area in 1950 and extended citizenship to Palestinians living there. During this period, the Gaza Strip was under Egyptian military administration. In the 1967 war, Israel captured and occupied these areas, along with the Sinai Peninsula (from Egypt) and the Golan Heights (from Syria).

Israel established a military administration to govern the Palestinian residents of the occupied West Bank and Gaza. Under this arrangement, Palestinians were denied many basic political rights and civil liberties, including freedom of expression, freedom of the press and freedom of political association. Palestinian nationalism was criminalized as a threat to Israeli security, which meant that even displaying the Palestinian national colors was a punishable act. All aspects of Palestinian life were regulated, and often severely restricted by the Israeli military administration. For example, Israel forbade the gathering of wild thyme (za'tar), a basic element of Palestinian cuisine.

Israeli policies and practices in the West Bank and Gaza have included extensive use of collective punishments such as curfews, house demolitions and closure of roads, schools and community institutions. Hundreds of Palestinian political activists have been deported to Jordan or Lebanon, tens of thousands of acres of Palestinian land have been confiscated, and thousands of trees have been uprooted. Since 1967, over 300,000 Palestinians have been imprisoned without trial, and over half a million have been tried in the Israeli military court system. Torture of Palestinian prisoners has been a common practice since at least 1971, and dozens of people have died in detention from abuse or neglect. Israeli officials have claimed that harsh measures and high rates of imprisonment are necessary to thwart terrorism. According to Israel, Palestinian terrorism includes all forms of opposition to the occupation (including non-violence).

The Settlement Issue

Israel has built hundreds of settlements and permitted hundreds of thousands of its own Jewish citizens to move to the West Bank and Gaza, despite that this constitutes a breach of international law. Israel has justified the violation of the Fourth Geneva Convention and other international laws governing military occupation of foreign territory on the grounds that the West Bank and the Gaza Strip are not technically "occupied" because they were never part of the sovereign territory of any state. Therefore, according to this interpretation, Israel is not a foreign "occupier" but a legal "administrator" of territory whose status remains to be determined. The international community has rejected the Israeli official position that the West Bank and Gaza are not occupied, and has maintained that international law should apply there. But little effort has been mounted to enforce international law or hold Israel accountable for the numerous violations it has engaged in since 1967.

Jerusalem

The UN partition plan advocated that Jerusalem become an international zone, independent of both the proposed Jewish and Palestinian Arab states. In the 1948 Arab-Israeli War, Israel took control of the western part of Jerusalem, while Jordan took the eastern part, including the old walled city containing important Jewish, Muslim and Christian religious sites. The 1949 armistice line cut the city in two. In June 1967, Israel captured East Jerusalem from Jordan and almost immediately annexed it. It reaffirmed its annexation in 1981.

Israel regards Jerusalem as its "eternal capital." Arabs consider East Jerusalem part of the occupied West Bank and want it to be the capital of a Palestinian state. . . .

UN Security Council Resolution 242

After the 1967 war, the UN Security Council adopted Resolution 242, which notes the "inadmissability of the acquisition of territory by force," and calls for Israeli withdrawal from lands seized in the war and the right of all states in the area to peaceful existence within secure and recognized boundaries. The grammatical construction of the French version of Resolution 242 says Israel should withdraw from "the territories," whereas the English version of the text calls for withdrawal from "territories." (Both English and French are official languages of the UN.) Israel and the United States use the English version to argue that Israeli withdrawal from some, but not all, the territory occupied in the 1967 war satisfies the requirements of this resolution.

For many years the Palestinians rejected Resolution 242 because it does not acknowledge their right to national self-determination or to return to their homeland. It calls only for a just settlement of the refugee problem. By calling for recognition of every state in the area, Resolution 242 entailed unilateral Palestinian recognition of Israel without recognition of Palestinian national rights.

Camp David I

After coming to power in Egypt in late 1970, President Anwar Sadat indicated to UN envoy Gunnar Jarring that he was willing to sign a peace agreement with Israel in exchange for the return of Egyptian territory lost in 1967 (the Sinai Peninsula). When this overture was ignored by Israel and the US, Egypt and Syria decided to act to break

the political stalemate. They attacked Israeli forces in the Sinai Peninsula and the Golan Heights in October 1973, on the Jewish holy day
of Yom Kippur. The surprise attack caught Israel off guard, and the
Arabs achieved some early military victories. This prompted American political intervention, along with sharply increased military aid to
Israel. After the war, US Secretary of State Henry Kissinger pursued
a diplomatic strategy of limited bilateral agreements to secure partial
Israeli withdrawals from the Sinai Peninsula and the Golan Heights
while avoiding negotiations on more difficult issues, including the fate
of the West Bank and Gaza. By late 1975 these efforts had exhausted
their potential, and there was no prospect of achieving a comprehensive Arab-Israeli peace settlement.

In late 1977, Sadat decided to initiate a separate overture to Israel.
His visit to Jerusalem on November 19, 1977 led to the Camp David
accords and the signing of an Egyptian-Israeli peace treaty in 1979.

In September 1978, President Jimmy Carter invited Sadat and Israeli
Prime Minister Menachem Begin to Camp David, a presidential retreat
in Maryland. They worked out two agreements: a framework for peace
between Egypt and Israel, and a general framework for resolution of
the Middle East crisis, i.e. the Palestinian question.

The first agreement formed the basis of the Egyptian-Israeli peace
treaty signed in 1979. The second agreement proposed to grant autonomy to the Palestinians in the West Bank and the Gaza Strip, and
to install a local administration for a five-year interim period, after
which the final status of the territories would be negotiated.

Only the Egyptian-Israeli part of the Camp David accords was implemented. The Palestinians and other Arab states rejected the autonomy concept because it did not guarantee full Israeli withdrawal
from areas captured in 1967 or the establishment of an independent
Palestinian state. In any case, Israel sabotaged negotiations by continuing to confiscate Palestinian lands and build new settlements in
violation of the commitments Menachem Begin made to Jimmy
Carter at Camp David.

The Palestinian Resistance Movement and the First *Intifada*

By John R. Gee

After the 1948 war between Israel and the surrounding Arab countries, a substantial Arab refugee population was created. These people had fled their homes as the Israeli army occupied various regions beyond the boundaries allotted to Israel by the United Nations. Many of these Palestinians ended up in either the territory that became known as the West Bank or in the Gaza Strip, living in hastily erected refugee camps. In this excerpt from his book Unequal Conflict, *author John R. Gee explores how the Palestinian resistance movement emerged from this refugee experience and how it eventually led to the violent uprising known as the first* Intifada. *Gee is the senior information officer at the Council for the Advancement of Arab-British Understanding.*

In the course of the 1948 war, expelled Palestinians normally fled to the nearest accessible Arab-controlled territory. Sometimes, the subsequent advance of the Israeli army meant that they had to move a second or third time. Those forced out of the Galilee region mainly went to Lebanon or Syria; Palestinians in the central part of the country generally fled to what became known as the West Bank, apart from those who lived in Jaffa: surrounded by Jewish-inhabited territory and Zionist military forces, most fled by sea, ending up in Lebanon. In the south-west, Palestinians crowded into the shrunken region under Egyptian control which became known as the Gaza Strip. A few, richer or with helpful personal contacts, travelled further afield. . . .

At first, the expelled Palestinians believed that their exile would be brief. They looked to those with far more power than them to secure their rights. On 11 December 1948, the United Nations General Assembly passed Resolution 194, which included the statement that:

> the refugees wishing to return to their homes and live at peace with their neighbours should be permitted to do so at the earliest practicable date, and that compensation should be paid for the property of those choosing not to return and for the loss of or damage to property.

The UN has reaffirmed that resolution annually, but it has never been backed by measures to ensure Israeli compliance. Neither did it seem that the Arab regimes defeated in the 1948 war would do anything effective in their support. Young Palestinian intellectuals from among the expelled tired of waiting and resolved to act.

The Arab Nationalists' Movement

Some saw their best hope for the future lying in political change in the wider Arab world. The communist parties, which called for radical political and social change, attracted few. Their ideology was objectionable to many in a society in which the influence of religion was strong and they had, in any case, condemned themselves irreparably in the eyes of the great majority by their support for the partition resolution in 1947. Ba'athism, which claimed to combine pan-Arabism [the movement to unite Arabs from all countries under a single cause] with socialism, won a few adherents. Palestinians were instrumental in founding the Arab Nationalists' Movement (ANM). Its leading figure was George Habash, a doctor by profession, whose family were Christians from Lydda, expelled when that city fell to Israeli forces in 1948. Habash and other Palestinians in the ANM saw Arab unity as the key to winning the liberation of Palestine. They considered that the failure of the Arab armies against Israel in 1948 was mainly due to the nature of the Arab regimes, which they saw as corrupt, pro-imperialist entities which were solely concerned with looking after their own selfish interests and those of their foreign masters. They believed that [Egyptian president Abdel Gamal] Nasser had shown the way forward when he took control of the Suez Canal, confronted Britain and France, carried out internal social and economic reforms and, particularly, when he sought to encourage Arab unity: a united Arab world under a popular nationalist government could surely mobilise the resources to defeat Israel. After the 1967 war, the Palestinian ANM members joined with two other groups to establish the Popular Front for the Liberation of Palestine (PFLP).

Fatah

Others took a very different view. They gravitated towards the group which emerged at the end of the 1950s as al-Fatah, a name derived from the (reversed) Arabic acronym of the Palestinian National Liberation Movement. Yasser Arafat emerged as first among equals in Fatah's leadership. . . .

Fatah believed in the desirability of Arab unity, but thought that it was more likely to be realised through the struggle to liberate Palestine than as a precondition for undertaking that struggle. It also believed that differences over questions such as whether Palestine should develop on socialist lines should not be allowed to take precedence over the need to unite around the central objective of the liberation of Palestine. This 'Palestine first' approach allowed Fatah to embrace a wide range of views within its ranks, from leftists who believed in a clearly defined two-stage advance to socialism, via national liberation, to bourgeois Palestinians who contributed generously to its finances and were none too keen on any notion of class warfare. Fatah believed that the Palestinians had to win back control of their own destiny and this could only be done if they organised themselves for the liberation of their homeland, rather than relying on others to restore their rights to them.

Fatah argued that armed struggle was the only way to liberate Palestine. It did not expect that the Palestinians would defeat Israel on their own, but believed that they could do so with strong Arab allies and international support. Fatah believed that, before long, Israel would go to war against the neighbouring Arab states and defeat them. The discredited regimes would fall, to be replaced by popular nationalist governments ready to make a wholehearted commitment to support the Palestinian struggle. However, Fatah considered that the Palestinians should not allow themselves to be drawn into the internal politics of the Arab countries: this would only divert their energies from their central mission. Fatah's views on armed struggle changed over the following decades, but its commitment to Palestinian independent decision making and to non-interference in the affairs of Arab states remained steady, even if events forced it off course at times. . . .

The armed struggle was launched on the night of 31 December 1964–1 January 1965. The operation, directed against an Israeli scheme to divert water from the Jordan, was announced in a communique issued in the name of 'Al Assifah' (The Storm). Fatah preferred not to admit responsibility for its first attacks until it was confident that the armed struggle had been successfully launched, but, once it did, it still used the name 'Al Assifah' in communiques to refer to its armed forces.

The Six-Day War

In June 1967, the fateful clash which Fatah had foreseen took place. After a period of rising tension, Israel launched a devastating surprise attack on Egypt, Jordan and Syria. It destroyed most of their air forces on the ground, thereby securing total mastery of the air within hours of the conflict beginning. Within six days, Israel crushed the armies of its Arab opponents and conquered the West Bank and Gaza Strip, as well as Egypt's Sinai Peninsula and Syria's Golan Heights. This debacle plunged the Arab world into gloom. It could not be viewed in the same light as the defeat of the Arab armies in 1948 under the corrupt old regimes. Particularly shocking was the fact that Egypt, under the nationalist leadership of President Nasser and deeply popular throughout the Arab world, had been defeated so quickly and decisively.

Fatah decided to relaunch the armed struggle as quickly as possible following the 1967 war. Its hope was to escalate the conflict in the newly-occupied Palestinian territories until it developed into a popular uprising. Organisers, including Arafat, infiltrated into the West Bank with relative ease, re-establishing links with Fatah activists and winning new recruits. Armed operations re-commenced in August 1967, but did not unfold as hoped. Israeli counter-measures were extremely effective and the great majority of West Bank Palestinians felt they had too much to lose by engaging in a violent conflict with Israel. Fatah's guerrilla networks were smashed and Arafat himself barely escaped back to Jordan. The armed struggle (save in the Gaza Strip over the next three years, where the PFLP managed to conduct a more sustained guerrilla campaign) now became one mainly fought on the borders of Israeli-controlled territory. The relative weakness of the government of Jordan following the 1967 war allowed Palestinian guerrillas the opportunity to establish bases there, from which they mounted hit and run attacks across the river Jordan. Israel responded by shelling and bombing alleged 'terrorist bases'. On 21 March 1968, it made a large scale ground assault upon guerrillas in the Jordan valley town of Karameh.

The Fidai'in

In his writings on 'people's war' [Chinese leader] Mao Zedong had advised that, in the face of an attack by superior enemy forces, the revolutionary fighters should retreat and give battle when conditions favoured them, rather than risking heavy losses to their own forces. Fatah's leadership knew that an Israeli attack was coming and it was familiar with Mao's advice, but decided that its guerrillas should stay in Karameh and fight. This was an example of the tactical shrewdness it has often displayed. It believed that the advantages to be gained by demonstrating that its forces were ready to confront the Israelis would

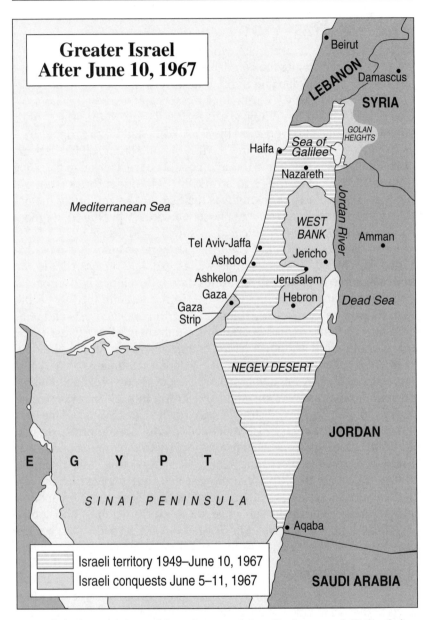

**Greater Israel
After June 10, 1967**

Beirut

LEBANON

Damascus

SYRIA

GOLAN
HEIGHTS

Haifa

Sea of
Galilee

Nazareth

Mediterranean Sea

WEST
BANK

Jordan River

Amman

Tel Aviv-Jaffa

Ashdod

Jericho

Ashkelon

Jerusalem

Gaza

Hebron

Dead Sea

Gaza
Strip

NEGEV DESERT

JORDAN

E   G   Y   P   T

SINAI PENINSULA

Aqaba

| | Israeli territory 1949–June 10, 1967 |
| | Israeli conquests June 5–11, 1967 |

SAUDI ARABIA

outweigh the anticipated loss in casualties. So it proved. Palestinian losses were heavy, but the Israeli attackers retreated with about 25 dead and their mission of liquidating the guerrillas unaccomplished. They left behind tanks disabled by Jordanian artillery fire, which were towed in triumph through Amman. Fatah celebrated the outcome as a victory, and so it was seen throughout the Arab world.

Thousands of volunteers, including non-Palestinians, hurried to join the fidai'in ('men who sacrifice themselves'—the Arabic term commonly used for the fighters). The majority joined Fatah, but others turned to rival organisations such as the PFLP. The relationship between the Palestinian national movement and the Arab states was transformed. Such was the popularity of the Palestinian resistance that it was politically advantageous to take a strong public stance in its support. Some Arab states created fidai'in organisations which were aligned with them, notably Saiqa (backed by Syria) and the Arab Liberation Front (backed by the Iraqi Ba'athist regime).

The Birth of the PLO

The growth of Palestinian political activism had impelled the Arab states to support the establishment of the Palestine Liberation Organisation (PLO) in 1964. Ahmad Shuqairy, who had previously served as a diplomat, became Chairman of the PLO Executive Committee, the organisation's highest post. National institutions were set up from above, including the General Union of Palestinian Workers (now Palestine Trade Union Federation), General Union of Palestinian Women and the Palestine Liberation Army, a conventional military force whose units were placed under the control of the Arab states in which they were based.

This was essentially a means for keeping Palestinian nationalist activity within strictly defined bounds, acceptable to most Arab states. As such, it was treated with some scorn by Fatah, but that attitude changed in the post-Karameh conditions. With popular support and the backing of a previously suspicious Nasser, Fatah was able to secure a majority in the Palestine National Council (PNC—the body responsible for determining the policy of the PLO and electing its leadership) and PLO Executive Committee in 1969. It might have chosen to allow the PLO to wither away and stressed its own leading role at this point, but chose to take over and work through the established machinery. The PLO had a representative role acknowledged by the Arab states, and it seemed advantageous to build upon that. In addition, the PLO offered a framework within which Fatah could work with other Palestinian organisations rather than attempt to create a new one with them. . . .

Within a very short space of time, the Palestinian resistance movement achieved a great deal. It reasserted the existence of the Palestinian Arabs as a people with their own identity and a cause which they believed to be just. It restored a sense of dignity and pride to them. The tenacity with which, during the trials of the following years, the Palestinians—especially those in the camps—maintained their support for the PLO is a tribute to what the movement headed by Fatah accomplished after the 1967 war. . . .

The First Intifada

[Over the next twenty years, the PLO struggled to gain relevancy among the international community. In 1987, an event occurred that solidified its position.] An Israeli truck collided with two vans carrying Palestinian labourers returning to the Gaza Strip from working in Israel. Four Palestinians were killed and seven injured. Rumours spread that this was not an accident, but a deliberate attempt to kill Palestinians. The following day, 9 December 1987, young stone-throwing Palestinians clashed with Israeli soldiers in Jabalya refugee camp, near Gaza City; 15-year-old Hatem al-Sisi was shot dead, the first 'martyr' in the Intifada. Demonstrations rapidly spread throughout the Gaza Strip and West Bank. They became mass confrontations with the occupation forces whose violent reaction failed to suppress them. Something new, something astonishing was happening in Palestine.

The Intifada was a spontaneous popular uprising, neither planned nor anticipated by the PLO or the Islamic organisations which were starting to play a more prominent role in Palestine. It took them by surprise, as well as Israel, which found itself in the unaccustomed position of being placed on the defensive by the Palestinians. The people living under occupation had simply had enough of their treatment at Israel's hands. At the forefront of the street protests were young Palestinians who had grown up under Israeli occupation, witnessing parents humiliated at check-points and in searches, seeing an alien army on their streets and certain that they had nothing to look forward to while the occupation continued. Many felt they had nothing to lose, and that partially explains the fearlessness which many older Palestinians said that they displayed.

A popular uprising does not last long on a spontaneous basis. To sustain revolt, leadership and organisation are required. Both were forthcoming, thanks to the work done by Palestinian organisations within the West Bank and Gaza Strip over the previous ten years or so. . . .

The Organization of Revolt

A United National Leadership of the Uprising (UNLU) was established by the four main PLO groupings inside Palestine (Fatah, PFLP, DFLP [Democratic Front for the Liberation of Palestine] and PCP [Palestine Communist Party]). It issued its first communique on 8 January 1988, after which they appeared in a steady stream until the end of the Intifada, normally roughly at two-week intervals. They were produced in leaflet form and slid under doors, pasted on walls or handed out by activists throughout the West Bank and Gaza Strip. They commented on current events, set forth Palestinian demands and called for actions by Palestinians, particularly strike days. Their importance was clear to all. They were prepared by the UNLU in consultation with the PLO leadership abroad. This showed the limits to the initiative allowed to the internal leaders: they could not simply act on the basis of the known political positions of the PLO, but had to consult with the external leadership about the political statements and demands they made. Security came second to this requirement: exchanges over the texts of UNLU communiques took place via fax machines and telephones, so that Israel had a pretty good idea of who the UNLU leaders were and what their next communique would demand.

The Intifada was the greatest struggle mounted within their homeland by the Palestinians since the 1936–39 revolt. It brought into action women and young people on a scale unknown before in Palestine. As an energetic mass movement, it probably lasted between 18 months and two years, after which it lost momentum and tended to settle into something of a routine sustained by organisation and UNLU calls, finally petering out in 1992.

The Uprising showed the world that the Palestinian people as a whole absolutely rejected Israel's occupation of the West Bank and Gaza Strip. It shook the Israeli occupation regime, had a demoralising effect on the army and made ruling the West Bank and Gaza Strip cost Israel money (instead of being a net income yielder). The majority of Israeli political leaders (not only those of the Zionist left) were forced to recognise that the existing relationship between Israel and the Palestinians would have to change, although for most, this meant seeking a way of perpetuating overall Israeli control without having to deploy Israeli soldiers throughout Palestinian residential areas in order to do it. . . .

The Gulf War

Political gains from the Intifada might have been greater but for events which took place far from Palestine's borders. The Soviet bloc crumbled away during the first three years of the Intifada, knocking out one of the pillars of the PLO's diplomatic strategy. Then, in August 1990, President Saddam Hussein of Iraq sent the Iraqi army into Kuwait and annexed it. In the ensuing conflict between Iraq and the US-led coalition which aimed to turf it out of Kuwait, there was no doubt where the sympathies of the vast majority of Palestinians lay. Wishful thinking seemed to prevail over common sense; there was a widespread belief that Iraq would win. When the air war began, credence was given to wildly exaggerated Iraqi claims of coalition airplanes downed; once the truth that the coalition had total control of the skies had sunk in, many clung to the belief that the Iraqi army would perform well in the ground war. Its comprehensive rout came as another shock.

The consequences of having taken this attitude were catastrophic. The Arab states of the Gulf took their revenge on the Palestinians [for supporting Saddam Hussein] by cutting off financial support to the PLO and expelling the great majority of their Palestinian residents, most of whom had not shared their compatriots' enthusiasm for the Iraqi dictator. As these communities had given generously to the PLO and were often sending money to support families in the West Bank, Gaza Strip, Jordan, Syria or Lebanon, this was a devastating double blow. Conditions deteriorated rapidly for millions of Palestinians. The PLO could not operate as before: an elaborate structure built and maintained over more than 20 years and dependent upon generous infusions of Arab oil money began to disintegrate. Families of martyrs found the financial support they had previously received drying up; money which the PLO had dispensed to its constituent organisations was no longer forthcoming, so their own institutions went into crisis; PLO offices, established as the result of efforts which had brought the PLO wider diplomatic relations than the State of Israel in the 1980s, one by one closed down except for those regarded as the most important. In addition, some public sympathy was temporarily lost in the West: the Palestinians were seen to have taken a hypocritical stance of wanting human rights and self-determination for themselves, while supporting a dictator who denied them to Kuwaitis and Kurds, besides treating many Iraqi Arabs in the most brutal way.

Palestinian reasons for supporting Iraq in the Gulf crisis varied. They included resentment towards oil rich states which Palestinians felt should do more to support them, and sympathy for Saddam Hussein because he had made statements declaring his determination to stand up to Israel at a time when the rest of the Arab world appeared to prefer a supine posture. The main motivation seems to have been opposition to Western (especially US) action against fellow Arabs. Because they had seen the United States arm Israel, bolster its economy and shield it against international efforts to make it respect Palestinian rights and disgorge the territories it occupied in 1967, opposition to action in the Arab world by the USA came naturally. Some Palestinians (still very much a minority) have since concluded that their stand in the Gulf crisis was mistaken, but even they are divided between those who think it was wrong in principle and the ones who simply regard it as a tactical error.

The PLO had, at the outset, criticised Iraq's invasion of Kuwait and called for a negotiated solution to the crisis, but aligned itself with Iraq in opposing the US-led coalition. On this occasion, there was no doubt that it was in tune with Palestinian popular feeling. It would have been wiser not to have been and to have tried to inject a bit of realism into the popular mood, but it shared in the illusions and sentiments of the people.

Had it built its demands for Palestinian rights on universal principles rather than an appeal to specific UN resolutions favouring the Palestinians, it might have kept its bearings better in this crisis and taken a stand that was not only more principled, but tactically advantageous too.

The End of the Uprising

The Intifada had rescued the PLO leadership from marginalisation and strengthened its hand in pursuing diplomatic gains for the Palestinian cause: Jordan had officially relinquished all claim to the West Bank and the USA had even been induced to open a direct dialogue with it for a few months. As the dust of the Gulf War settled, it found itself facing similar challenges to those confronting it before the Intifada, but was more poorly equipped to meet them. The Soviet bloc had vanished and some powerful Arab states were angry with the PLO, severely undercutting its diplomatic strategy. The PLO's 'state in waiting' apparatus was collapsing under the impact of financial crisis, but to make matters worse, the leadership was far weaker. Israeli assassination had taken a toll of experienced Palestinian leaders during the previous 25 years, but at the beginning of the Intifada, three of Fatah's founders—Yasser Arafat, Abu Jihad and Abu Iyad—still stood at the head of the PLO. Abu Jihad, deputy military commander, was assassinated in his home in Tunis in a Mossad/army operation on 16 April 1988, four months after the Intifada broke out. Abu Iyad, head of security and an influential political voice, was gunned down by a member of the anti-PLO group led by Abu Nidal (and long sponsored by Iraq) on 14 January 1991, hours before the expiry of the UN ultimatum to Iraq to withdraw from Kuwait. The death of these veterans deprived the PLO of leaders who had wielded considerable authority in their own right and whose opinions carried great weight with Arafat, whose tendency to concentrate power in his own hands and make policy decisions without prior reference to the responsible PLO bodies became virtually unrestrained, save only by his sense of what the Palestinians would accept.

Arafat's own health was deteriorating. With events seeming to conspire against him and the organisation he headed, he accepted the terms imposed upon the Palestinians as a precondition for their participation in the Madrid Middle East peace conference in 1991. When the talks which followed became bogged down, he engaged in secret diplomacy without the consent or knowledge of the PLO's leading bodies to agree to terms for a settlement with Israel. This was the background to the ceremony which took place on the White House lawn on 13 September 1993, when [Israeli prime minister Yitzhak] Rabin and Arafat signed the Declaration of Principles.

The Oslo Accords
Fail to Bring Peace

By Baylis Thomas

In September 1993 the historic Oslo Peace Accords were signed by PLO leader Yasser Arafat, Israeli prime minister Yitzhak Rabin, and Israeli foreign minister Shimon Peres, creating a road map for peace that would span the next decade and include the return of land to the Palestinians in exchange for peaceful relations. For the first time since the 1967 war, peace looked possible between Israelis and Palestinians.

In the following selection Baylis Thomas describes the events surrounding the Oslo accords. He reports that while the accords were considered an important step toward peace, both sides were dissatisfied with the agreement. In November 1995 the peace process faltered when Rabin was assassinated by a fundamentalist Jew. After Rabin's assassination, violence escalated on both sides of the conflict.

In November 1999 the Oslo process resumed, but by May 2000 negotiations had stalled again. A formal summit was arranged at Camp David between U.S. president Bill Clinton, Israeli prime minister Ehud Barak, and Yasser Arafat, now the Palestinian president. Opinions differ regarding the details of the summit (very little of what was discussed was officially recorded), but the outcome showed little progress past the initial Oslo Accord. On September 28, 2000, Israeli Likud Party leader and soon-to-be prime minister Ariel Sharon made a controversial visit to the Haram al-Sharif Temple Mount, which helped to spark the start of the Al-Aqsa Intifada (second Intifada). This new wave of violence made peace seem increasingly unlikely as the twenty-first century dawned.

Thomas is a freelance journalist and clinical psychologist. This selection is excerpted from his book How Israel Was Won: A Concise History of the Arab-Israeli Conflict.

Baylis Thomas, *How Israel Was Won: A Concise History of the Arab-Israeli Conflict*. Lanham, MD: Lexington Books, 1999. Copyright © 1999 by Lexington Books. Reproduced by permission.

The Gulf War demonstrated that Isarel's security lay in technological defense against missile attack from distant soils, not in
acquiring more land in the immediate vicinity (i.e., the West Bank).
Nevertheless, after the war, Israel continued spending billions of dol-
lars for expropriation and settlement of the occupied territories in the
name of security, infuriating President [George H.W.] Bush and his
secretary of state James Baker. Prime Minister [Yitzhak] Shamir demanded $10 billion from the United States for even more settlements
but Bush faced him down.

Secretary Baker attempted to control settlement expansion by spon-
soring talks among Israel, the Arab states and Palestinians (a non-PLO
delegation, including Hanan Ashwari, Faisal Husseini and Rashid Khalidi) dealing with interim forms of autonomy in the occupied territories. Ten international conferences (the "Madrid Conferences") were
held between late 1991 and the middle of 1993. In the midst of these
talks, a Rabin/Labor government was elected on a platform promising
peace with the Palestinians in a year.

Yet [Prime Minister Yitzhak] Rabin remained Israel's tough "security man" concerning the territories. As he put it, "Security takes precedence over peace"—that is, control takes precedence over negotiation.
In pursuit of that control over the occupied territories, Rabin devoted
large sums for "strategic settlements" in "security areas" comprising
about one-half of the West Bank, with $600 million spent on con-
struction of interconnecting roads in 1994. The prime minister also authorized the continued construction of 10,000 housing units for Jews
only in the Arab–East Jerusalem section of the West Bank. By these
actions Rabin brought the Madrid talks to a point of crisis in November 1992. The Palestinians were outraged, claiming that Israel would
effectively control two-thirds of the West Bank. Then, in early 1993,
Rabin deported 416 alleged Hamas activists—an act that discredited
the talks and galvanized Palestinian extremists. Thirteen Israelis were
murdered a month later by terrorists and Rabin completely sealed off
Israel from the occupied territories.

The Oslo Peace Accords

Initially, Rabin had little interest in some informal, secret, Jewish-
Palestinian talks taking place in Oslo. But after the Madrid talks col-
lapsed, Rabin had greater need to find a way to fulfill his campaign
pledge of peace. Moreover, talks with Syria about conditions for Israeli withdrawal from the Golan Heights—a strategy proposed by
Ehud Barak (Israeli Defense Force (IDF) Chief of Staff) to draw the
Arab countries together in order to isolate and weaken the bargaining
power of Palestinians—had gone nowhere. There were other reasons

why Rabin reconsidered the Oslo talks. [Yasser] Arafat, the key, was personally in a weak position. His declaration of a Palestinian state had been ignored by the West and he was persona non grata with President Bush. He had also lost the support of the collapsing Soviet Union and had provoked the anger of Saudi Arabia over his position on the Gulf War. Rabin saw that Arafat was at serious disadvantage as a negotiator and that the Palestinians, exhausted by the intifada, might now be willing to come to favorable terms. "It became clear that the PLO was bankrupt, divided and on the verge of collapse and therefore ready to settle for considerably less," [according to historian Avi Shlaim].

Rabin threw Arafat a life line with little risk to himself and potential gain for Israeli security—Arafat's secular PLO might conceivably be able to suppress Islamic terror groups. After eight months of secret talks, an agreement was reached—the *Oslo Peace Accords.*

What the United States called a "historic breakthrough," Palestine National Council (PNC) member Edward Said called "a Palestinian Versailles" and Israel's Amos Oz characterized as "the second biggest victory in the history of Zionism." On the surface, the Oslo Accords looked benignly helpful to the Palestinian cause regarding self-determination. Agreed upon was the "Declaration of Principles on Interim Self-Government Arrangements" (DOP). This was not so much a set of agreements as an *agenda* for negotiations. However, some things were agreed: There was to be a *transfer of power* to Palestinians for an *interim* period. Palestinians would be permitted to administer unto themselves in five spheres: health, social welfare, direct taxation, education/culture and tourism. After two months, Israel would withdraw from Gaza and Jericho, redeploying troops to surrounding areas. The PLO would train a police force for local, internal Palestinian security though Israel would remain responsible for overall security in the West Bank and Gaza. It was also agreed that within nine months, a *Palestinian Council* would be elected by Palestinians to take over administrative functions for the PLO. Within two years, discussions would begin concerning a *permanent* settlement to be enacted in five years, a settlement separate from any agreements made during the interim period.

For the Palestinians, exhausted by the intifada and brutalized by the occupation, the idea of gaining even limited autonomy with partial IDF withdrawal was a cause for celebration. On the other hand, for Palestinian leaders outside the Arafat camp—for example, Dr. 'Abd al-Shafi, a Madrid negotiator, and PNC member Edward Said—the primary disappointment of the Oslo Accords was their failure to address the fundamental issue of Palestinian *sovereignty* over the West Bank and Gaza. Palestinian territorial rights were never mentioned, even as a negotiable item on the agenda. Nor did the Accords place any restrictions on the continued building of Jewish settlements and their interconnecting road networks—that is, further erosion of Palestinian territory (some 65 percent of the West Bank already under Israeli control).

Clearly, the Accords were possible only because negotiations about all the difficult and important issues relating to the Israeli-Palestinian conflict were excluded. Sovereignty, Jewish settlements, Palestinian refugee return and East Jerusalem were all off-limits. Rather, the central focus of the Oslo Accords was on the *security of Jewish settlements and Israel* and the requirement that the PLO suppress Islamic militants as a precondition for withdrawal of Israeli troops from certain Palestinian areas.

The Recognition Letters

The most important feature of the Oslo Accords, for detractors and supporters alike, was not the DOP provisions for limited autonomy/self-rule, but the *preamble letters* that conferred mutual recognition on the PLO and Israel. Nabil Shaath, Arafat's close advisor and negotiator, found in these recognition letters a parity between the two sides. Said saw the opposite—no parity where Palestinians had no power from which to negotiate, where "mutual" recognition was really *unilateral* recognition.

It is true that in this exchange of letters Arafat gave away much, Rabin little. Arafat affirmed: (1) PLO recognition of Israel's right to exist in peace and security; (2) renunciation of the Palestinian Covenant; (3) acceptance of UN Resolutions 242 and 338 (despite their omission of Palestinian territorial rights); (4) renunciation of the use of terrorism and other acts of violence; and (5) assumption of overall responsibility for the behavior of PLO elements and personnel. In exchange, Rabin gave to Arafat recognition that the PLO represented the Palestinian people with whom Israel would negotiate. That is, Arafat recognized both the Jewish State and its right to security while Rabin recognized Arafat as an agent for a collection of people without a state or a similar right to security. Ignored outright was the Palestinian state declared five years earlier and recognized by over 100 countries—a nullity in the Accords.

Palestinian Critiques of the Accords

Arafat's recognition of Israel had, in the opinion of some Palestinian scholars, given away, wittingly or unwittingly, explicitly or implicitly, a number of important and fundamental Palestinian legal rights:

(1) Arafat's recognition of and agreements with Israel constituted

an admission that Israel *rightfully* possessed powers in the territories which it was empowered or entitled, through the Oslo Accords, to *transfer*, at its discretion, to the Palestinians. Such right of power does conflict with accepted international opinion concerning Israel's legal status as an occupier of conquered territories—occupiers do not possess powers which they can legally transfer to the occupied. If Israel had practiced *de facto* sovereignty over the territories since 1967, Arafat now seemed to be conferring on Israel *de jure* sovereignty. In this respect, Israel became the rightful possessor of powers, some of which Arafat hoped might be transferred to the Palestinians. "We have," declared 'Abd al-Shafi, "helped to confer legitimacy on what Israel has established illegally."

(2) Arafat's admission of Israeli rights and powers in the territories also seemed to have the effect of undermining the Palestinians' right of appeal to international courts for protection normally afforded people under occupation. Such protections include the Fourth Geneva Conventions, the Hague Conventions and other international laws prohibiting use of life-threatening force and torture, prohibiting settlement of occupied territories, etc.—conventions and laws systematically violated in the territories before and after the Accords. To cast off occupier status seemed to undermine the occupied's right to international appeal.

(3) Another criticism of the Accords was that recognition of Israel constituted a recognition of Israel's *laws*, including martial law in the territories. These laws, still in force, have in fact led to expropriation of land and water imposition of taxes and deportation of inhabitants.

(4) The clause about Israel's "right to exist in peace and security" has also been construed as an Israeli right to remedy any situation it deems threatening to security—for example, reintroduction of troops or undercover agents into self-rule areas to handle settler-Palestinian conflicts or apprehend suspected terrorists.

(5) But the central Palestinian criticism of the Oslo Accords involves Arafat's commitment to Israel's peace and security. This commitment made him responsible for Palestinian terrorism, future intifadas or other violence directed at Israelis. Israel assumed no parallel responsibility for IDF or settler violence directed at Palestinians. Moreover, Arafat's pledge to end violence set him squarely against Hamas and Islamic Jihad, thereby creating conditions for potential civil war within the Palestinian community. As historian Avi Shlain noted, this was a Rabin strategy "aimed at playing the Arabs off one against the other in order to reduce the pressure on Israel to make concessions."

With Arafat "on the ropes" (as Rabin appraised) and Hamas "flourishing" (as Israeli intelligence reported), it was unlikely that Arafat could accomplish what Israel had not during the previous six years— suppression of dissident Islamic terrorists. Certainly, suicide bombings would be impossible to prevent. Consequently, Rabin had available to him seemingly justified grounds for halting negotiations whenever Arafat failed (predictably) to fulfill his commitment to Israeli security. Moreover, given Israel's continuing land expropriation, exclusion of Palestinian labor from Israel, collective punishment and Shin Bet (Secret Service) operations in the Palestinian police, Arafat's chance of suppressing dissident Palestinian terrorism could only worsen.

Rabin's Goals

What was Rabin's ultimate goal in signing the Oslo Accords? Was he, like Shamir, toying with Palestinians in endless talk about autonomy while confiscating land in the cause of Greater Israel—maintaining the status quo? Or seeking the *appearance* of peacemaker without much risk or cost? Or was he seeking to shift responsibility for terrorism onto Arafat to discredit him? Did he actually think that Arafat could deliver on Israel's security?

Certainly Rabin was following Shamir's classic fait accompli strategy of expansion in the West Bank and, like Shamir, avoiding the issue of Palestinian sovereignty. And yet Rabin did *not* want to incorporate two million West Bank and Gazan Palestinians into Israel by annexing the occupied territories. He once favored the 1967 Allon Plan whereby Israel would annex Jewish settlement areas and the Jordan Valley (eastern side of the West Bank) but not the densely populated Palestinians areas better controlled by Jordan—the once-popular "Jordanian option." Certainly, he and the Israeli public wanted to be rid of the Gaza Strip, a sealed-off, packed prison of angry unemployed Palestinians that, in his view, might best "sink into the sea." Turning responsibility for the Gaza Strip over to the PLO was certainly one of Rabin's goals. Hence, the defensible conclusion of Israeli researcher Meron Benvenisti that Oslo was a device to enable the Israelis to gradually evacuate "precisely those [dense Palestinian population areas] they were keen to get rid of." In any event, Arafat accepted the Gaza offer and, needing to show Palestinians that he could bargain for a foothold and symbolic concession in the West Bank, demanded and received Jericho as well.

But Rabin's goal may finally have been one of *separation*, in which West Bank Palestinians were to end up in a dozen, small, densely populated "self-rule" enclaves militarily encircled and effectively walled off from Israel. This plan, described below, was announced in January of 1995, the year of Rabin's assassination.

In sum, Rabin accomplished through the Oslo Accords a number of goals on the main issues: (1) PLO recognition of Israel's power and ultimate security responsibilities over all the occupied territories; (2) PLO acquiescence to continued settlement-building on rapidly diminishing amounts of land; (3) PLO responsibility for halting Palestinian terrorism and suicide bombings; and (4) PLO responsibility for the Gaza Strip. The rest of the Accords concerned protracted negotiations over secondary issues about the exact timing, meaning and extent of limited Palestinian autonomy.

Oslo II

Two years after the 1993 Oslo Accords when the Palestinians were on their own (their former guardian, Jordan, had signed a peace treaty with Israel in 1994), the Palestinians and Israelis made further interim agreements. Dubbed "Oslo II," or the Taba agreements, these agreements were designed to slowly extend Palestinian self-rule to other towns and villages besides Gaza and Jericho. This plan, if and when completed, was to give administrative and police control (not sovereignty) to Palestinians over about 3 percent of the West Bank (called Area A). Another 24 percent (Area B) was to have a Palestinian administration with joint Israeli/Palestinian military control. The remaining 73 percent, comprising Israeli "public" lands, settlements, army camps and roads, was to remain under exclusive Israeli control. Hebron, a city of 120,000 Palestinians and 400 Israelis, posed a special case in which Israel was to retain part control of the city. The accords also allowed for construction of a system of internal roadblocks that could prevent north-south Palestinian travel in the West Bank and entry into East Jerusalem.

To summarize the agreements of Oslo I and II: (*a*) Palestinians have administrative authority to control health, social welfare, direct taxation, education/culture, tourism and policing in limited areas of the West Bank and Gaza; (*b*) Israel has responsibility for security over all the West Bank and Gaza and exclusive control of and authority for the security of all Jewish settlements and settlers even when in Palestinian self-rule (A) areas, (*c*) Israel has veto power over all laws drafted by the Palestinian Council; (*d*) Israel's occupier laws remain in force throughout the West Bank and Gaza, (*e*) all Palestinian administrative appointments require Israeli approval; (*f*) Israel has the exclusive power to collect customs fees and to tax locally produced Palestinian goods; (*g*) Israel controls all commercial and personal traffic between Gaza and the West Bank and between the West Bank, Israel and Jordan; and (*h*) Israel controls all exits and entries to Palestinian self-rule areas and controls all roads.

The Faltering Peace Process

As previously described, Arafat's failure to assure Israel's security (a violation of the Oslo Accords) could be expected to threaten self-rule negotiations. On the other hand, were he to successfully suppress Hamas, he would alienate Palestinians sympathetic to Hamas and jeopardize his own political base. Were Arafat more popular his dilemma would be less. But some Palestinians have seen Arafat as a dictator who has merely replaced Israel's military governor. And the PLO has been criticised as a corrupt patronage system in which members indulge in luxurious living amidst the people's poverty. Arafat's strong-armed police force, charged with keeping the peace, has been accused of doing Israel's "dirty work"—torturing and killing Palestinians in pursuit of Islamic dissidents. If Arafat works for Israeli and not Palestinian security, his popular support erodes.

Moreover, Hamas has enjoyed begrudging respect from more than 20 percent of Palestinians. Many have rejected Hamas's terrorist acts and seen its Islamic ideology as intolerant and undemocratic. Yet Hamas has also exhibited concern for the people, delivering food, clothes, money and jobs to poor Palestinians. [As commentator Neil MacFarquhar writes], "Many downtrodden Gazans depend on Hamas charity to feed their children—a consideration for Mr. Arafat if he were to crack down hard as Israel demands." The people, in "existential crisis, demoralized, depoliticized and depressed . . . facing a cavernous void," [according to Norman Finkelstein in *The Rise and Fall of Palestine*], admire the fact that Hamas and Islamic Jihad have at least *acted* against IDF and settler violence.

Arafat's dilemma: he gains a degree of popular support by making progress on Israeli withdrawal, but if that requires open civil war with Hamas and Islamic Jihad, he also loses some support. Hanan Ashrawi believes that, "The more the PLO shows it can deliver on the Israelis' principle demand—security—the less it is accepted by its own people." Israel and Hamas both understand Arafat's bind—they know that it is not as simple as Israel alleges, that Arafat is a terrorist sympathizer, nor as simple as Hamas alleges, that Arafat is an Israeli collaborator.

The Peace Process Is Destroyed

In November 1995, two months after Oslo II, Rabin was assassinated by a Jewish religious fundamentalist, an act dramatizing the intense differences between orthodox and secular groups in Israel. Shimon Peres took over the premiership and called for early elections in the summer of 1996. In a close vote, Peres lost to Likud's Benyamin Netanyahu, who had campaigned on a platform seeking to nullify the "dangerous" Oslo Peace Accords. Terrorist bombings provided an election boost for Netanyahu's no-accommodation position.

Netanyahu has been described [by Serge Schmemann] as having been "waiting all along for a way to get out of an arrangement he always held in disdain." Like Rabin, security has been seen by him as a product of strength rather than peace negotiations and his disdain has been linked not only to a "deep-seated distrust of the Oslo peace agreement [but also] of the Arabs," [Schmemann notes]. Netanyahu's writings suggest a "vision of the Jew as perennial target who can never entrust his security to anyone, who must surround himself with what [Vladimir] Jabotinsky called a 'steel wall.'"—that making peace with Arabs is like "keeping fish in a glass bowl until they learn not to bump against the glass," [according to Schmemann].

Foreign minister David Levy has criticized the prime minister for "destroying the peace" through actions seemingly designed to scuttle the Accords. These have included: tunnel-building in Jerusalem; a massive housing project at Har Homa; a dam project on Syria's doorstep; the delayed Oslo II deployment of Israeli forces from self-rule areas; the punishment of Palestinians through harsh economic sanctions; the withholding of Palestinian tax monies from the Palestinian Authority; and the sealing off of Israel from Palestinian labor and goods. These actions could be expected to fuel Palestinian anger and only add to Arafat's inability to control terror. Some have wondered whether Netanyahu has been the indirect source of the terrorism that he has used to disparage Palestinians and freeze withdrawal negotiations.

The prime minister did make a concession in early 1997 of withdrawing the IDF from three-quarters of Hebron (virtually an all-Arab town). At the same time, his approval of the rapid expansion of Jewish housing at Har Homa (southern Jerusalem in the West Bank), some 6,500 new units in April 1997, drew condemnation from the UN General Assembly. Netanyahu declared: "We shall build in Jerusalem and everywhere, no one will deter us." His plan was to enlarge Jerusalem to half again its current size and build many more Jewish homes in Har Homa by the year 2000 despite U.S. disapproval. Netanyahu followed the same expansionist track as Rabin and Peres who together increased settlements by 49 percent during their four-year rule.

Suicide bombings in Jerusalem in the summer of 1997 brought the "peace process" to a halt. Netanyahu refused negotiations about withdrawal and held Arafat responsible. Arafat accused Netanyahu of a "plot to stop and destroy the agreements." Their mutual recriminations involved a circular linkage in which suicide bombings lead to halted negotiations which in turn lead to more suicide bombings. The United States has favored Netanyahu's side: [In January 1997, the U.S. State Department declared that], "Only if the Palestinian side proves itself able and willing to comply with its security responsibilities is Israel obligated to transfer additional areas in the West Bank to Palestinian jurisdiction"—confirmation to the terrorists that bombings are effective in sabotaging negotiations seen as submission to Israel.

Settler violence in the occupied territories worsened after the 1993 Accords. Settlers feared that limited self-rule would compromise what they considered rightful Jewish sovereignty over all of Palestine. Clashes accelerated. A settler massacred twenty-nine Palestinian worshippers in Hebron in February 1994. This was followed by the killing of thirty Arabs by the IDF, ushering in a wave of revenge suicide bombings by Hamas. In January 1997, when settlers in Hebron brandished Uzi sub-machine guns and laid claim to Palestinian land, eight protesting Palestinians were shot by an off-duty IDF soldier. Two months later fifty-eight Palestinians were shot by the IDF during a demonstration over Israeli construction at Har Homa. The Israeli government has been no more able or willing to curb the violence of the IDF, undercover agents or extremist settlers than has Arafat been able or willing to curb Islamic extremists. . . .

The Middle East Conflict Continues

Given the future prospects for Palestinians, Palestinian terrorism cannot be expected to end. In that sense, the Middle East conflict is *not* over. As long as any Palestinian is willing to kill an Israeli and himself in protest or frustration over statelessness, injustice and poverty, Israel will have a security problem. And as long as any settler, Shin Bet operative or Israeli soldier is willing to kill a Palestinian for God, country or retaliation, Palestinians will have a security problem. As long as both Palestinians and Jews terrorize and are terrorized by "sacrificers" against injustice and loss, Hamas and [religious Zionist group] Gush Emunim alike, a *mutual* local security problem will remain. Attempts to stop terrorism through infliction of collective punishment or through bestowal of limited self-rule seem to have only fueled the problem. Nor has Israeli assassination of Palestinian figures such as Abu Jihad or Yahya Ayyash accomplished more than provoke counter-attack—as when, in March 1996, Hamas ended its self-imposed ceasefire. Palestinian terrorism cannot be punished away any more than could Jewish terrorism be punished away by the British in 1946–1948. "It is not easy to get a conquered person to resign himself to defeat," [as Maxine Rodinson writes in *Israel: A Colonial-Settler State*]. Nor does moral condemnation work. When violence is the last bargaining chip of those feeling oppressed, it elicits little guilt. So as long as local terrorism persists . . . the Middle East conflict is not over.

The Four Wars of
Israel and Palestine

By Michael Walzer

According to Michael Walzer, a coeditor of the political journal Dissent *and the author of this article, Israelis and Palestinians are not fighting a single war but are instead engaged in four distinct conflicts at the same time. These four wars are: the Palestinian war to destroy the state of Israel, the Palestinian war for an independent state that would coexist with Israel, the Israeli war for security within the established 1967 borders, and, finally, the Israeli war to expand and control the current Israeli state, including the settlements and occupied territories. In order to understand the Israel-Palestine conflict, it is necessary to first understand these four key components. Walzer explores each of these unique wars and then looks at how they affect each other and build the greater conflict.*

The great simplifiers are hard at work, but Israel/Palestine has never been a friendly environment for them, and it is especially unfriendly today. They are bound to get it wrong, morally and politically, and that is a very bad thing to do, for the stakes are high. There isn't one war going on in the Middle East, and there isn't a single opposition of right and wrong, just and unjust. Four Israeli-Palestinian wars are now in progress.

- The first is a Palestinian war to destroy the state of Israel.
- The second is a Palestinian war to create an independent state alongside Israel, ending the occupation of the West Bank and Gaza.
- The third is an Israeli war for the security of Israel within the 1967 borders.
- The fourth is an Israeli war for Greater Israel, for the settlements and the occupied territories.

It isn't easy to say which war is being fought at any given moment;

Michael Walzer, "The Four Wars of Israel/Palestine," *Dissent*, vol. 49, Fall 2002, pp. 26–33. Copyright © 2002 by Dissent Publishing Corporation. Reproduced by permission.

in a sense, the four are simultaneous. They are also continuous; the wars go on even when the fighting stops, as if in confirmation of [political theorist] Thomas Hobbes's definition: "For war consisteth not in battle only, or the act of fighting, but in a tract of time wherein the will to contend by battle is sufficiently known. . . ." Throughout the course of the Oslo peace process, some Palestinians and some Israelis were fighting the first and fourth of these wars—or, at least, were committed to fighting them (and their will to contend was sufficiently known so that it could have been dealt with). The actual decision to restart the battles was taken by the Palestinians in September 2000; since then, all four wars have been actively in progress.

Different people are fighting each of the four wars at the same time, side by side, though the overall emphasis falls differently at different times. Our moral and political judgments have to reflect this complexity. Taken separately, two of the wars are just and two are unjust. But they don't appear separately in the "real world." For analytic purposes, we can begin by looking at them one by one, but we won't be able to stop there.

The War Against Israel

This is the war that is "declared" every time a terrorist attacks Israeli civilians. I believe that terrorism always announces a radical devaluation of the people who are targeted for random murder: Irish Protestants in the heyday of the Irish Republican Army, Europeans in Algeria during the National Liberation Front's (FLN) campaign for independence, Americans on September 11, 2001. Whatever individual terrorists say about their activities, the intention that they signal to the world, and above all to their victims, is radical and frightening: a politics of massacre or removal or of overthrow and subjugation. Terrorism isn't best understood as a negotiating strategy; it aims instead at total victory, unconditional surrender. The flight of a million and a half Europeans from Algeria was exactly the sort of victory that terrorists seek (the FLN was helped in its project, it should be remembered, by terrorists on the European side).

Israel's Jewish citizens have to assume that something similar is what Palestinian terrorists are seeking today: the end of the Jewish state, the removal of the Jews. The language of incitement—the sermons in Palestinian mosques, the funerals where the "martyrdom" of suicide bombers is commemorated, the slogans shouted at political demonstrations, the celebration of terrorists as heroes in schools run by the Palestine Authority (PA)—makes this intention clear, and it is the explicit goal of the leading terrorist organizations, Hamas and Islamic Jihad. But can it be called the goal of the Palestinian liberation movement taken as a whole? Is this what Yasir Arafat is really after? It isn't easy to read him; he may think that he is using the terrorists; he may even hope one day to kill or exile them as the Algerian government did to its terrorists in the aftermath of independence. But clearly, whatever his ultimate intentions, he is right now a supporter or at least an accomplice of terrorism. . . . His distancing gestures, the occasional arrests, and the perfunctory condemnations after each attack long ago ceased to be convincing; he cannot be surprised if ordinary Israelis feel radically threatened. This first war is real war, even if it looks right now like a losing war with terrible consequences for the Palestinian people and even if some (or many) Palestinians believe themselves to be fighting a different war.

The War for an Independent State

This is the war that leftist sympathizers in Europe and America commonly claim that the Palestinians are fighting, because they think that this is the war the Palestinians should be fighting. And some (or many) of them are. The Palestinians need a state. Before 1967, they needed a state to protect them against Egypt (in Gaza) and Jordan (on the West Bank); since 1967, they need a state to protect them against Israel. I have no doubt about this, nor about the Palestinian right to the state they need, even though I believe that the original seizure of the West Bank and Gaza was justified. In 1967, the Arabs were fighting a war of the first kind on my list, against the very existence of Israel. There was no occupation in those days; Egyptian publicists talked openly of driving the Jews "into the sea." But the territories that Israel controlled at the end of its victorious defense were supposed to be used (this is what its leaders said at the time) as bargaining chips toward a future peace. When, instead, the government sponsored and supported settlements beyond the old border (the green line), it conferred legitimacy on a resistance movement aimed at liberation. And the longer the occupation went on, the more settlements proliferated and expanded, the more land was expropriated and water rights seized, the stronger that movement grew. It is worth recalling how peaceful the occupation was in its early days, how few soldiers it required when it was believed, on both sides, to be temporary (and when war number one had been decisively defeated). A decade later, Prime Minister Menachem Begin denied that there was any such thing as "occupied territory"; the whole land was the Land of Israel: the government adopted the ideology of conquest and settlement. And the occupation was far more onerous, far more oppressive when its reality was denied than when it was called by its true name.

So it is certainly a legitimate goal of Palestinian militants to establish a state of their own, free of Israel—and of Egypt and Jordan too. The first intifada (1987), with its stone-throwing children, looked like a struggle for a state of this kind, limited to the West Bank and Gaza, where the children lived. It was not exactly a nonviolent struggle (though it was sometimes described that way by people who weren't watching), but it did show discipline and high morale, and its protagonists seemed to acknowledge limits to their struggle: it wasn't intended to threaten Israelis on their side of the green line, where most Israelis lived. And that is why it was successful in advancing the peace process—though Palestinian leaders subsequently declined, so it seems to me, to gather the fruits of their success.

The renewed intifada that began in the fall of 2000 is a violent struggle, and it is not confined to the Occupied Territories. Still, the interviews that journalists have conducted with many of the fighters suggest that they (or some of them) consider themselves to be fighting to end the occupation and force the settlers to leave; their aim is an independent state alongside Israel. So this second war is a real war too, though again it isn't clear that Arafat is committed to it. Does he want what some, at least, of his people certainly want: a small state alongside a small (but not as small) Israeli state? Does he want to trade in the aura of heroic struggle for the routine drudgery of state-building? Does he want to worry about the water supply in Jericho and the development of an industrial zone in Nablus? If the answer to these questions is yes, then we should all hope that Arafat gets what he wants. The problem is that many Israelis, who would share this hope if they were hopeful about anything, don't believe, and don't have much reason to believe, that the answer is yes.

The War for Israeli Security

It is unclear how many Israeli soldiers think that this is the war they are fighting, but the number is certainly high. The reserve call-up that preceded the March–April 2002 Israeli "incursions" into West Bank cities and towns produced a startling result. Usually the army calls up about twice the number of soldiers that it needs; the routine pressures of civilian life—sick children, infirm parents, school exams, trouble at the office—are accepted as excuses; lots of reservists don't show up. In March 2002, more than 95 percent of them did show up. These people did not believe that they were fighting for the occupied territories and the settlements; all the opinion polls show a massive unwillingness to do that. They believed that they were fighting for their country or, perhaps better, for their safety and survival in their country. The 95 percent response was the direct product of the terrorist attacks. It is possible, of course, that Sharon exploited the fear of terrorism in order to fight a different war than the one his soldiers thought they were fighting. Still, whatever the war in Sharon's mind, a substantial part of the Israeli army was defending the country against the terrorist threat. The third war is a real war and, morally, a very important war: a defense of home and family in the most immediate sense. But some Israeli homes and families are located on the wrong side of the green line, where their defense is morally problematic.

The War for the Occupied Territories

The Israeli right is definitely committed to this war, but the support they have in the country is (again) uncertain. Prime Minister Ehud Barak at Camp David in 2000 believed that he would win a referendum for an almost total withdrawal, if this were part of a negotiated settlement of the conflict as a whole. Withdrawal under pressure of terrorist attacks probably does not have similar support, but that tells us nothing about the extent of support for the occupation and the settlements; it tells us only that Palestinian terrorism is a political disaster for the Israeli left. In the face of terror, the left cannot mobilize opposition to the settlements; it finds itself marginalized; its potential supporters are more and more skeptical about its central claim: that withdrawal from the territories would bring a real peace. And that skepticism opens the way for right-wing politicians to defend the settlements—which are no different, they argue, from cities and towns on the Israeli side of the green line: if we don't fight for Ariel and Kiryat Arbah (Jewish towns on the West Bank), we will have to fight for Tel Aviv and Haifa.

But the fight for Ariel and Kiryat Arbah guarantees that there won't be a real peace. For the settler movement is the functional equivalent of the terrorist organizations. I hasten to add that it is *not the moral equivalent*. The settlers are not murderers, even if there are a small number of terrorists among them. But the message of settler activity to the Palestinians is very much like the message of terrorism to the Israelis: we want you to leave (some groups on the Israeli right, including groups represented in Sharon's government, openly support a policy of "transfer"), or we want you to accept a radically subordinate position in your own country. The settlers' aim is Greater Israel, and the achievement of that aim would mean that there could not be a Palestinian state. It is in this sense only that they are like the terrorists: they want the whole thing. They are prepared to fight for the whole thing, and some Israelis presumably believe that that is what they are doing right now. The fourth war is a real war. The vote of the Likud in May 2002 to bar any future Israeli government from accepting a Palestinian state suggests a strong commitment to continue the occupation and enlarge the settlements. Still, I suspect that most of the reservists called up in March, or those who are now (August) patrolling Palestinian cities, would not be prepared to fight for those goals if they thought that this was the only war in which they were engaged.

It was the great mistake of the two center-left prime ministers, Yitzhak Rabin and Barak, not to set themselves against the settler movement from the beginning. They thought that they would most easily defeat the right-wing supporters of Greater Israel if they waited until the very end of the peace process. Meanwhile they compromised with the right and allowed a steady growth in the number of settlers. If, instead, they had frozen settlement activity and chosen a few isolated settlements to dismantle, they would have provoked a political battle that I am sure they would have won; and that victory would have been definitive; a gradual out-migration of settler families from the territories would have begun. Failing that, Palestinian radicals were able to convince many of their people that compromise was impossible; the conflict could have only one ending: either the Palestinians or the Israelis would have to go. . . .

The Order of Importance

How can we adjudicate among the four wars? What kind of judgments can we make about whom to support or oppose, and when? A lot depends on the questions I have not answered: how many Israelis, how many Palestinians, endorse each of the wars? Or, perhaps better, we might ask: what would happen if each side won its own just war? If the Palestinians were able to create a state on their side of the green line, would they (or a sufficient majority of them) regard that as the fulfillment of their national aspirations? Would they accept that kind of statehood as the end of the conflict, or would the new state sponsor an irredentist politics and secretly collude in an ongoing terrorist war? Arafat's behavior at Camp David and after doesn't suggest a hopeful answer to these questions. Similarly, does the Israeli defense of statehood stop at the green line, or does the current government's conception of state security (or historical destiny) require territories beyond that, even far beyond that? Sharon's behavior since coming to power doesn't suggest a hopeful answer to this question. . . .

I put war number one, for the destruction of the state of Israel, ahead of war number two, for statehood in the territories, because it appears that statehood could have been achieved without any war at all. And I put the war for Greater Israel after the defensive war for Israeli security because the previous Israeli government was prepared to renounce territorial "greatness" entirely. But if the Palestinians make a serious effort to repress the terrorist organizations, and if that effort does not move the Sharon government to rethink its position on the territories, then these orderings would have to be revised. In any case, all four wars are now in progress: what can we say about them?

Ending the Wars

The first war has to be defeated or definitively renounced. Critics of Israel in Europe and at the United Nations have made a terrible mistake, a moral as well as a political mistake, in failing to acknowledge the necessity of this defeat. They have condemned each successive terrorist attack on Israeli civilians, often in stronger language than Arafat has used, but they have not recognized, let alone condemned, the succession itself, the attacks taken together, as an unjust war against the very existence of Israel. There have been too many excuses for terrorism, too many efforts to "understand" terror as a response (terrible, of course) to the oppressiveness of the occupation. It is likely, indeed, that some terrorists are motivated by personal encounters with the occupying forces or by a more general sense of the humiliation of being occupied. But many other people have responded differently to the same experience: there is an ongoing argument among Palestinians (as there was in the IRA and the Algerian FLN) about the usefulness and moral legitimacy of terror. Palestinian sympathizers on the European left and elsewhere should be very careful not to join this argument on the side of the terrorists.

Winning the second war, for the establishment of a Palestinian state, depends on losing or renouncing the first. That dependence, it seems to me, is morally clear; it hasn't always been politically clear. If there ever is a foreign intervention in the Israeli/Palestinian conflict, one of its goals should be to clarify the relationship of the first and second wars (and also of the third and fourth). The Palestinians can have a state only when they make it clear to the Israelis that the state they want is one that stands alongside Israel. At some point, a Palestinian leader (it is unlikely to be Arafat) will have to do what [Egyptian president] Anwar Sadat did in 1977: welcome Israel as a Middle Eastern neighbor. Since Israel already exists, and Palestine doesn't, one might expect the welcome to come from the other direction. Perhaps it should; at some point, certainly, the welcome must be mutual. But the extent of the terror attacks now requires the Palestinians to find some convincing way to repudiate the slogan that still echoes at their demonstrations: "Kill the Jews!"

The relation of the third and fourth wars is symmetrical to that of the first and second: war number four, for Greater Israel, must be lost or definitively renounced if war number three, for Israel itself, is to be won. The March–April 2002 attacks on West Bank cities, and the return of Israeli soldiers to those same cities in June–July, would be much easier to defend if it was clear that the aim was not to maintain the occupation but only to end or reduce the terrorist threat. In the absence of a Palestinian war on terror, an Israeli war is certainly justifiable. No state can fail to defend the lives of its citizens (that's what states are for). But it was a morally necessary prelude to that war that the Sharon government declare its political commitment to end the occupation and bring the settlers home (many of them, at least: the actual number will depend on a negotiated agreement on final borders for the two states). Perhaps UN officials would have condemned the Israeli war anyway, whatever the government's declared commitments, but the condemnations could then have been seen as acts of hostility—not to be confused with serious moral judgments. As it was, the fierce argument about the massacre-that-never-happened in Jenin obscured the real moral issue, which was not the conduct of the battles but the political vision of the government that ordered them. The conduct of the battles seems to have conformed to the standards of just war theory, though the use of air power (for example, against the Gaza apartment house in July [2002]) has not always done so. The current occupation of Palestinian cities and the practice of collective punishment impose unjustifiable hardships on the civilian population. In battle, however, the Israeli army regularly accepted risks to its own men in order to reduce the risks that it imposed on the civilian population. The contrast with the way the Russians fought in Grozny, to take the most recent example of large-scale urban warfare, is striking, and the crucial mark of that contrast is the very small number of civilian casualties in the Palestinian cities despite the fierceness of the fighting. But the legitimacy of Israeli self-defense will finally be determined by the size of the "self"—the extent of the territory—that is being defended.

The General Plan

Almost everybody has a peace plan: one peace for the four wars. And everybody's plan (leaving aside those Palestinians and Israelis who are fighting for the whole thing) is more or less the same. There have to be two states, divided by a border close to the green line, with changes mutually agreed upon. How to get there, and how to make sure that both sides stay there once they get there—on these questions the disagreements are profound, between Palestinians and Israelis and also within both groups. Except in the most general terms, I cannot address these questions. The general terms are clear enough: Palestinians must renounce terrorism; Israelis must renounce occupation. In fact, neither renunciation seems likely given the existing leadership of the two sides. But there is a significant peace movement in Israel, and several political parties committed to renunciation, and among the Palestinians, though no comparable movement exists, there are at least small signs of opposition to the terror attacks. Perhaps whatever forward movement is possible must come independently from the two sides and, first of all, from outside what we used to call the "ruling circles.". . .

Ultimately, the partisans of wars two and three must defeat the partisans of wars one and four. The way to peace begins with these two internal (but not necessarily uncoordinated) battles. An American or American/European-sponsored truce would help the moderates on both sides, but, at the same time, the success of the truce depends on the strength of the moderates. Right now, it is hard to judge whether the "reform" of the Palestinian Authority would increase that strength. All good things don't come together in political life: some of the most moderate Palestinians are among the most corrupt, while the suicide bombers are no doubt idealists. Democratic elections in Palestine may well play into the hands of nationalist and religious demagogues; this is a real possibility in Israel too. Still, a more open politics among the Palestinians would allow public expressions of support for a compromise peace, and that would be a major advance.

Would it help to bring in an international force, under UN auspices, to police the (temporary or permanent) lines between Israel and Palestine? This is an increasingly popular idea, but it raises difficult questions about reciprocity. The Israeli settlers would have to be defeated before any such force came in, because the border along which it was deployed would certainly exclude many of the existing settlements. But the Palestinian terrorists would not have to be defeated, because they sit comfortably on one side of the line. It is easy to predict what would happen next: terrorists will slip through the UN's multinational patrols and kill Israeli civilians. Then Israel will demand that UN soldiers go after the terrorist organizations, which, since that would involve a major military campaign, they would refuse to do. And what then? An international force prepared to use force (and accept casualties) might well bring peace to the Middle East, but I cannot think of any country that is seriously prepared to commit its soldiers to actual battles. The UN's record in Bosnia, Rwanda, and East Timor is appalling. So, the only force likely to be deployed is one organized for peacekeeping, not peace-making, and then its effectiveness will depend on the previous victory of Israeli and Palestinian moderates. Internationalization is no substitute for that victory, and it is certainly doomed to failure if it follows upon the victory of Israeli moderates only.

Peace Through International Pressure

There is a form of international engagement, more ideological and political than military, that could he genuinely helpful. It is critically important to delegitimize the terrorists and the settlers. But this has to be done simultaneously and with some modicum of moral intelligence. The current boycott campaign against Israel, modeled on the 1980s campaign against South Africa, aims at a very one-sided delegitimation. And because the other side isn't led by an organization remotely like the African National Congress, or by a man remotely like Nelson Mandela, the success of this campaign would be disastrous. It would strengthen the forces fighting the first war. Only when European critics of Israel are prepared to tell the Palestinians that there will be no help for a PA complicit in terrorism, can they ask American critics of the Palestinians to deliver a parallel message to the Israeli government. Intellectuals committed to internationalism can best serve their cause by explaining and defending the two messages together.

I have tried to reflect the complexity of the Israeli/Palestinian conflict. I cannot pretend to perfect objectivity. The Israeli nationalist right, even the religious right, is a familiar enemy for me, whereas the ideology of death and martyrdom endorsed by so many Palestinians today is alien; I don't understand it. So perhaps someone else could provide a more adequate account of the four wars. What is crucial is to acknowledge the four. Most commentators, especially on the European left, but also on the Jewish and Christian right here in the United States, have failed to do that, producing instead ideological caricatures of the conflict. The caricatures would be easy to ridicule, if they did not have such deadly effects. For they encourage Palestinians and Israelis to fight the first and fourth wars. Those of us who watch and worry about the Middle East have at least an obligation not to do that.

CHAPTER 2

The Causes
of Conflict

Fear Has Increased Israeli Support for Military Action

By Libi Oz

In this article, originally published in Contemporary Review, *Israeli university student and former sergeant in the Israeli army Libi Oz gives an account of how the ongoing conflict has affected the lives of Israeli citizens. She describes how the fear of random violence at the hands of Palestinian suicide bombers has changed the day-to-day activities of many Israelis. This fear has also caused many people who once argued for a peaceful resolution to switch their support over to increased military action.*

The author also looks at the changing attitudes among Israelis regarding their national obligation to serve in the army reserve. All young Israelis must do mandatory military service when they turn eighteen and then intermittent reserve duty afterward. The author notes that although some people are refusing to take their place among the reserves because of their political views, the overall percentage of citizens participating in the mandatory reserve program is increasing.

Finally, Oz provides a critique of the way Israel has been represented in the international media. She argues that Israel has been depicted negatively because of a general misunderstanding in the international community regarding some basic truths about the conflict.

A normal day in my life begins when I open my eyes and rush to see the morning newspaper. I anxiously check the headlines to see if I recognize anyone in the pictures of the previous day's terror victims. As I ride the bus to my university in Tel Aviv, I observe my fellow passengers for anyone suspicious. Upon arrival at the university, I pass through the well-guarded gate, and am invariably asked to open my bag. En route to class, I look for my friends. I can't help but won-der whether anyone was called into the army reserve during the night.

When we leave the library at the end of the day, my friends and I have a hard time deciding whether or not we should go out. We are constantly trying to come up with ideas of places to go where there are no crowds. We'll often decide that it is not worth risking our lives to go wandering around at the nearby mall. Like many other Israelis, I would rather spend the evening at home than risk going to a bar, club or restaurant.

While these small daily sacrifices may sound trivial in comparison with the situation presented by the media, I can't imagine that there are many readers who would want to live this lifestyle. To be denied the freedom of walking down the street without fear is a price that no civilian should have to pay. Taking one's little brother to a movie or one's grandmother to a supermarket, potentially exposes all concerned to a suicide bomber. Our routine includes sitting in traffic because the road was blocked when a suspicious bag was found at a bus stop. Fam-ily members frequently call one another just to make sure they have reached their destination safely.

This year [2002] Independence Day was one of the days that strongly expressed the mood here. On the one hand, you could see flags hanging out of cars, houses and stores all over the country. The demand for flags this year was double that of last year. On the other hand, not many people went out into the streets to celebrate. The fear of being in crowded places took over this time. I, personally, preferred going to a private, well secured party rather than worrying my mom by going to the usual, mass outdoor celebrations. The Palestinian ter-rorists, even if they didn't actually succeed in committing an act of ter-ror by planting a bomb or having a suicide bomber blow himself up in a crowded area, did wreck our celebrations. Compared to previous years, this was a sad Independence Day.

Political Views

Israelis want a return to normality. The legitimacy of the Palestinian cause does not justify terror. Nothing justifies terror. Israelis are en-raged. I believe that it was this rage that impelled the government to resort to military actions. I am sure that Palestinians are enraged too. The difference is that we are reacting in a controlled manner, focus-ing on targets that propagate terror. The Palestinians are reacting with terror. They are killing for the sake of killing; we are killing in order to stop recent killing.

Many young people have changed their political views because of this relatively new situation. The shift is astounding. Israelis who two years ago were left-wing activists are now heard to say that they no longer believe that there are moderate voices on the other side who genuinely seek a permanent, peaceful resolution to the conflict. The same soldiers and students who eight years ago, after Prime Minister [Yitzhak] Rabin's assassination, were nicknamed 'the candle children' and were known for their anti-war views, are now in a fever of tit for tat actions. The final goal, and that's what most people believe, is indeed peace, one way or the other. The opinions concerning the way to achieve that peace are divided into more or less two main groups (excluding radical points of view). One group says that we should continue to fight until the other side understands that it will achieve nothing by terrorism and will then go back to the negotiating table. The other group says that in order to achieve peace, we should evacuate all the areas conquered in 1967.

This second group is particularly interesting, since some of its supporters express their protest by refusing to serve in the army reserves in those areas. These people founded a new movement called 'Courage to Refuse—Combatant's Letter'. I quote from their statement: 'We understand now that the price of occupation is the loss of the IDF's [Israel Defense Forces] human character and the corruption of the entire Israeli society'. What they mainly claim is that a person is not required to risk his life for something he doesn't believe in. A large proportion of those who signed this letter are students. Their purpose in this letter is not only to assuage their own consciences, but to influence society as well. Though this protest is legitimate in a democratic country, the reactions it elicits are very emotional and sharp. Since the consensus concerning the need to serve in the army in Israel is very broad and strong (about 80 per cent of Israelis support this policy), Israeli society does not treat those who refuse to serve with respect. Statements like 'Traitors' and 'You are an embarrassment to this country' have been heard. One of the unusual responses came from the Minister of Education, who proposed that university professors who publicly supported those who refused to serve in the army be put on trial. Those who object to this phenomenon say that a country fighting for its existence cannot afford citizen-soldiers who refuse to do their army service. However, the fact is that the people who refuse to serve are a small group, whereas the majority of reserve soldiers (almost 90 per cent) did serve in their units when they were called up.

Around the university campus here in Tel Aviv, one can observe many new student organizations this year. One organization is calling for the establishment of new borders that will not include the areas conquered in 1967. Another one is an Israeli-Arab student organization that is protesting against government policy and identifies with the suffering of the Palestinians. These organizations represent a relatively small number of students, since not many believe that these policies will bring the war to an end.

Army Dilemmas

In this war, as in any war, some immoral actions have been carried out. How do 20-year-old boys deal with the constant interaction with Palestinian civilians? This is not simple. Young soldiers often have to face Palestinians, who depend on the salary they bring home from the Israeli side, and tell them that they can't cross the border because of the curfew. The soldiers sometimes feel that this is punishment enough for the Palestinians. Yet, those same soldiers know that there is a chance that perhaps one among those Palestinians is a terrorist; if that terrorist succeeds in crossing the border into Israel, and kills or wounds Israelis, it will have been because the soldiers failed in their job of protecting Israeli citizens. That thought is what makes this difficult job bearable. What keeps soldiers from breaking down under the tension and wearying routine is mostly hanging on to their army pals. They work together, taking care of each other and looking out for each other, which makes it easier for them to continue doing their often unpleasant duty and helps them pass the hours of night guard duty. Not many soldiers break down and request early release.

Soldiers repeatedly face dilemmas, trying to avoid violating human rights as part of the military action they are performing and at the same time, striving to accomplish the military mission they've been assigned to. This dilemma is, of course, not unique to Israeli soldiers. According to the IDF's statement of values, the value of tenacity in fulfilling a mission is the most important one (except in the case of orders that are clearly illegal, when one is obliged to disobey), and Israeli soldiers and officers adhere to the orders they get. However, frequently, the orders they are given may not be very specific. In those cases they must use their own judgement, relying on their own personal moral compass and using their own discretion.

With the reserve soldiers, the situation is a bit different. Since most of them are married, the decision to do reserve duty is not an easy one and is accompanied by fear and panic at home. I cannot describe the way I felt when I saw the long lines of buses waiting to take the reserve soldiers to the army. It felt like no men were left around.

The Motivation to Serve

The high motivation to serve stems principally from the idea that this war is 'a war for our home, a war over the future of our children'. The older, more mature reserve soldiers react to what they see and do differently from the regular soldiers who are doing their required military service. Some of the former adopt a 'mask' and treat military service as a role that they are playing. They disassociate from their real identity and concentrate mainly on the performance.

The motivation to serve in the army among teenagers about to be drafted has not declined as a result of the recent large military actions. About 55 per cent of them want to serve in combat units. Such high motivation is derived from strong solidarity in today's Israeli society and the broad consensus regarding the army. The army, as an 'army of the people', influences society and society influences the army. Teenagers are not overwhelmed by the recent increase in the number of soldiers who have been wounded or killed, since they believe that this war is necessary and requires their contribution.

Most Israelis believe that no massacre was committed in the West Bank town of Jenin. I personally heard soldiers who served there claiming that they did see some immoral acts taking place, but nothing that even came close to massacre. The pictures repeatedly shown on TV of the area destroyed is really only a small section of the refugee camp. The army has very high standards of respect and consideration for the lives of innocent civilians. It was for this reason that 23 of our own boys were killed in the fighting in Jenin. If we had no regard for the lives of innocent civilians, 23 sons, husbands and fathers would be at home with their families now. They were the price we paid for the high moral and ethical standards upheld during the fighting.

Some soldiers even claimed that they saw the Palestinians taking bodies that were already in the hospital out into the street, in order to display them to the foreign media. This is, in many ways, a war over world public opinion.

Israel in the Media

Israelis sometimes feel the picture the European media draws is unbalanced, since not enough explanations have been provided from our side. Many details and stories were not published abroad because Israel doesn't make enough of an effort to bring them to the notice of foreign reporters. For instance, after the attacks on the World Trade Center on September 11, 2001, Palestinians prevented coverage of their outpourings of happiness and their celebrations in the West Bank and Gaza. Similarly, many other facts that might have explained some of the pictures shown on TV, e.g. the fact that Palestinian terrorists use their children as human shields, are not provided.

Above all, Israelis feel that there is a basic misunderstanding regarding this war. In Europe, many people see the situation as strong Israelis attacking weak Palestinians, whereas Israelis see themselves as a little nation surrounded by deserts of hostile Muslim nations. This is also one of the factors in the difference between the way this war is presented in much of the European media and the way it is presented in Israel.

Despite all, our life goes on. From one suicide bombing to the other we pull ourself together and try to enjoy life. I would like to end this article with a few lines from a poem called 'The Silver Salver', written by our national poet, Natan Alterman:

Through wondering tears, the people stare.
'Who are you, the silent two?'
And they reply: 'We are the silver salver
Upon which the Jewish State was served to you'.
And speaking, fall in shadow at the nation's feet.
Let the rest in Israel's chronicles be told.

Israeli Settlements in the Occupied Territories Are a Principal Cause of Violent Conflict

By Geoffrey Aronson

The construction of Israeli settlements on lands that were seized from Arab landowners during the 1967 war is one of the primary issues at the heart of the current conflict. According to international law, it is illegal for a country to establish settlements in areas occupied by force. Furthermore, the United Nations has called on Israel, a member nation, to put a stop to its settlement program.

For the Israelis, the settlements are often seen as a buffer zone between major metropolitan areas in Israel and potential suicide bombers who might try to reach the more densely populated areas in order to cause maximum casualties. However, the Israeli settlements are often placed in such a way that they control important resources, such as water, which is scarce in many parts of the region. Many Palestinians see the settlements as a way of taking over these resources in order to make Palestinian existence more difficult.

In the following article, taken from the Journal of Palestine Studies, *author Geoffrey Aronson explores the theory that the existence of the settlements is one of the primary reasons for the current violence. He argues that Israel's settlement expansion policy could never coexist with the various attempts at peace. Because peace cannot be achieved while the settlements exist, Palestinian militants will continue to target them, creating a persistent environ-*

Geoffrey Aronson, "Settlements and the Al-Aqsa Intifada," *Journal of Palestine Studies*, vol. 31, Autumn 2000, pp. 127–30. Copyright © 2000 by Geoffrey Aronson. Reproduced by permission.

ment of fear for the residents of the settlement blocs. Aronson, an expert on Israel's occupation policies, is the editor of the Report on Israeli Settlement in the Occupied Territories, *which is published by the Foundation for Middle East Peace in Washington, D.C.*

The idea that the existence and expansion of Israeli settlements in the occupied territories were compatible with the march toward a historic Israeli-Palestinian peace was one of the central assumptions underlying the Oslo process. During the [1990s] successive Israeli governments of whatever political stripe have combined a settlement policy of relentlessly "creating facts on the ground" with a strategy of diplomatic engagement with the Palestinian national leadership, Yasir Arafat's PLO [Palestine Liberation Organization]. This anomalous combination was embraced by the United States, which dismissed an Israeli policy intended to cripple prospects for Palestinian sovereignty as merely a "complicating factor" in the negotiating process. It was warily tolerated by the PLO leadership itself, which proved unable to fashion a diplomatic framework to constrain Israel's ongoing settlement expansion, let alone roll back the status quo.

In contrast to their representatives, the people of the occupied territories—in Jinin and Nablus, Balata and Dahaysha, Hebron, and Khan Yunis—are forced to confront on a daily basis this contradiction at the heart of the Oslo process. To them, ever-expanding settlements, and the Israeli investments in related infrastructure and military deployment that follow in their wake, *matter.*

Settlements and the Al-Aqsa Intifada

The Palestinian rebellion that erupted in September 2000 has been fueled by the popular Palestinian belief that settlements and settlers are both the symbolic expression of Israeli intentions to deny them national self-determination and the practical obstacle to the peaceful and dignified conduct of a viable daily existence.

The instruments of settler of existence in the occupied territories—settlements, the roads connecting them with each other and with Israel, as well as the settlers themselves—are the principal context in which the violence of the [intifada] has taken place. During the [first year] of the intifada, thirty-five settlers have been killed in drive-by shootings and roadside ambushes in the West Bank and Gaza Strip. Everyday life in settlements, from sending children to school to trying to have a washing machine fixed by a technician who refuses to travel to these areas, has been profoundly changed by concerns for personal security and economic well-being.

"Our lives here have been absolutely transformed," explained a settler from Homesh in *Ma'ariv.* We know when we leave our homes, but we don't know when, if ever, we will return."

In Gilo, reported *Ha'Aretz*, "The bedroom door of Haim and Jeanne Yiflah is now blocked by sandbags. Their house overlooking the slopes of Bayt Jala, resembles a military dugout."

"We have succeeded in making the lives of the settlers difficult," explained Marwan Barghouti, leader of Fatah's [quasi-military militia] *tanzim* in the West Bank. "Their settlements have become military bunkers rather than homes. Our message is simple: The Israeli people will not feel secure for as long as they continue to occupy our territory."

The transformation in everyday settler life has been all the more remarkable because of the extraordinary absence of a sense of personal insecurity nurtured in the decades since 1967. With the exception of the 1988–93 uprising, Palestinian violence directed at settlers and settlements had been notable by its scarcity, ineffectiveness, and episodic nature—that is, until September [2000].

"However secure and eternal the settlers [in Gaza's Katif bloc] believe themselves to be," noted an August [2001] article in *Ha'Aretz*, "the fences surrounding their homes continue to grow . . . and the perimeters of settlements are now lined with concrete blocks. Visitors to the Katif bloc are greeted with this forbidding sight, which brings to mind the labor camps and army barracks of wartime Europe."

In February 2001, the IDF [Israel Defense Forces] published a map offering a vivid visual confirmation of the extent to which Palestinian attacks have forced settlers, and those who are charged with protecting them, to adjust to this new reality. The 1,200 kilometers of roads in the West Bank and Gaza Strip have been newly reclassified according to their danger to traveling settlers.

Settlers have long been prohibited from entering the Palestinians' areas A [territory given over to PA control at the completion of the Oslo peace talks]. New "rules of the road" published in February advise settlers not to enter areas B except when traveling on main roads, to avoid all contact with Palestinian police, to travel in vehicles equipped with a communications device and armored against stones (the cost of outfitting private cars to withstand gunfire is prohibitive; a special $50 million allocation for this purpose was announced in July [2001]), and to travel in convoys of at least two vehicles.

The Economic Impact

The economic effects of Palestinian attacks compete with concerns for personal security. The industrial area of Atarot in East Jerusalem has been all but emptied of Israeli businesses, and the nearby airport has been transferred from civilian management to the IDF. Ten percent of the 1,000 small- and medium-sized settlement-based businesses in the region north of Ramallah, which employ 30 percent of settlement residents, have closed permanently in the last year, and another 30 percent have stopped operating. Less than 10 percent have moved their operations to Israel.

Agriculture in Gaza's Katif bloc is being crushed under a load of debt that even emergency government advances have little hope of reducing. The situation in the Jordan Valley, which has suffered for years from a declining settler population due to economic hardship, has been exacerbated by the intifada. The three state-owned utilities of telephone, water, and electricity have threatened, for example, to disconnect the settlement of Yafit from their respective services if outstanding balances are not paid.

"The policy of the present government," noted a letter sent in September, 2000 by representatives of the region's 3,500 settlers to Knesset members, "is throwing the residents of the valley into a crisis the likes of which they have never known, and is causing departures from the region in numbers that only our honor and yours keep us from specifying in this letter."

One of the main tasks undertaken by the IDF during the intifada has been to "increase the sense of settlers' security" and to enable them to live a normal everyday existence. According to MK [member of the Knesset, the Israeli elected parliament] Ran Cohen of the opposition Meretz party, "Almost half the IDF is invested in defending [settlers] and their roads." Palestinian actions have made security along the 1,200 kilometers of West Bank roads the number one problem facing the IDF.

Settlement Roads

"Travel along roads in the territories can be described in one word," began a recent article in *Ma'ariv*, "fear."

In response to this situation, and in an attempt to restore the settlers' evaporating sense of personal security, the IDF has adopted a series of progressively draconian steps that have crippled everyday Palestinian life. In Gaza, for example, the IDF has completely separated the traffic patterns of both communities, to the Palestinian's disadvantage. The Oslo II provision for Israeli control of areas adjacent to roads has been extended from 75 to 300 meters. Palestinian use of more advanced weaponry may be answered by extending the perimeter of "clean" areas denuded of orchards and buildings around roads to almost one kilometer. The system of closures, road closings, checkpoints, and passive security measures, while in some cases improving settlers' sense of security, has severely restricted the movement of 3 million Palestinians cooped up in balkanized [broken up] islands, areas under nominal control of the Palestinian Authority (PA). Increasing IDF incursions into areas A have also been prompted in large part by the Palestinian policy of targeting settlements.

Thus, though Palestinians have succeeded in making the lives of settlers hell, in the last analysis it is a routine, manageable kind of hell punctuated by spasms of anticipated violence. The sense of insecurity has prompted thousands of settlers to return to Israel and has added to the difficulties of attracting new residents to settlements in a national economy plagued by recession and falling housing prices and demand. An investigation by *Ha'Aretz* revealed that 10,000 settlers—5 percent of the total in the West Bank and Gaza Strip—have left the territories this year, five times the typical annual emigration rate. These departures can pose critical social problems, especially in smaller settlements in the Jordan Valley and around Jinin, but after one year of armed Palestinian opposition during the last three decades, they do not in any fashion imperil the settlement enterprise.

Notwithstanding the population loss, the YESHA council [Council of the Settlements in the West Bank] announced an increase of 8.5 percent, or 17,000, in the settler population of the West Bank (excluding East Jerusalem) and Gaza Strip during [2000], up to 227,000. The investigation by *Ha'Aretz* suggests far more modest growth of less than 5 percent.

Fewer than one hundred armed Palestinians have been responsible for the havoc wreaked on settler roads. Hizballah [Lebanese terrorist organization] forces in Lebanon were also small in number, but that is where the similarity ends. The activity of Palestinian attacks on settlements and settlers represents not so much a strategy as an opportunistic, uncoordinated, and isolated exploitation of Israeli lines of communication by a small fraction of Palestinians under arms, a tactical instrument aimed at wearing down an enemy that shows no sign of abandoning the settlement enterprise rather than a persistent assault aimed at defeating it.

Although roadside attacks have been concentrated in a few areas, the armed forces associated with the PA have not been engaged in any coherent fashion in coordinated attacks on traveling settlers, let alone settlements. The shooting at settlements in Gaza, Hebron, Psagot, and even Gilo in East Jerusalem has been undertaken, at best, with only short-term tactical considerations in mind. Even on such a tactical level, it is difficult to establish the purpose for such actions beyond simply making life difficult for settlers.

Responses to Violence

To the terrible price Israel has exacted on Palestinians as a consequence of this effort must be added the rehabilitation of the settler community, which had been on the defensive since the beginning of the Oslo process, in Israel's domestic arena. Palestinian attacks on Gilo, which is viewed by Israelis as an unremarkable part of Jerusalem, and terror bombings throughout Israel proper have mobilized Israel's entire Jewish population on both sides of the Green Line [the boundary separating the warring factions], adding to the sense that "We're all in this together."

In the Palestinian community, few voices have been raised against shooting at settlers. "Israeli society is paying a heavy price as a result of the continuation of the Intifada and the unraveling of [Israeli] security and stability," observed Jamal Abu Samhadana, one of the founders of the popular resistance committees in Rafah. "This encourages the Palestinian public to carry on and support the struggle against the Israeli occupation." Yet the option of armed attacks of any sort appears to be under increasing critical scrutiny. "Only by political means shall we achieve our goals, by the use of rocks to fight the Israelis, on the roadblocks and in the settlements, not inside Israel, and not using firearms," noted a 2 August [2001] editorial by the Palestinian news agency WAFA. Photographs of Muslim worshippers throwing their shoes at Israeli soldiers during protests at Jerusalem's al-Aqsa Mosque, continued the editorial, "was more effective than mortar shells fired at Israeli settlements. The stone and the shoe are doing the job, and not the mortar shells."

Jihad Is the Only Way to Liberate Palestine

By Hamas

Hamas, a militant Palestinian political group that sprang up at the start of the first Intifada, *is calling for Muslims to participate in a jihad, or holy war, against the Israelis and their supporters. The group was formed to fight against the secularization of Arab countries, targeting Arab leaders who steered away from Islamic fundamentalism as the main underlying principle of government and moved toward more open societies. Hamas seeks to establish an Islamic Palestinian state on the land that Israel now occupies. One arm of the group uses standard political means to try to achieve this goal, establishing community organizations, educating children, and running for political offices. Another arm of Hamas, however, has been responsible for a large percentage of the suicide bombings against Israeli citizens since its formation, and its charter makes clear that violence is a necessary component of the struggle to displace Israel.*

Concentrated in the Gaza Strip and the West Bank, Hamas operates in opposition to Yasser Arafat's party, the Palestine Liberation Organization. However, the group has been known to work with the Palestinian Authority, the current Palestinian governing body, even though Hamas embraces terrorism and the two organizations ultimately seek different goals.

The viewpoint that follows is excerpted from the group's founding charter and illustrates the way in which its interpretation of the Koran, the holy text of Islam, drives them to embrace violence as a key tactic for attaining their goals. This fundamentalism is a major contributing factor to ongoing violence in the region.

Hamas, *Hamas Charter*, August 1988.

A rticle Six. The Islamic Resistance Movement is a distinct Palestinian Movement which owes its loyalty to Allah, derives from Islam its way of life and strives to raise the banner of Allah over every inch of Palestine. Only under the shadow of Islam could the members of all regions coexist in safety and security for their lives, properties and rights. In the absence of Islam, conflict arises, oppression reigns, corruption is rampant and struggles and wars prevail. . . .

Article Nine. Hamas finds itself at a period of time when Islam has waned away from the reality of life. For this reason, the checks and balances have been upset, concepts have become confused, and values have been transformed; evil has prevailed, oppression and obscurity have reigned; cowards have turned tigers, homelands have been usurped, people have been uprooted and are wandering all over the globe. The state of truth has disappeared and was replaced by the state of evil. Nothing has remained in its right place, for when Islam is removed from the scene, everything changes. These are the motives.

As to the objectives: discarding the evil, crushing it and defeating it, so that truth may prevail, homelands revert [to their owners], calls for prayer be heard from their mosques, announcing the reinstitution of the Muslim state. Thus, people and things will revert to their true place. . . .

Article Eleven. The Islamic Resistance Movement believes that the land of Palestine has been an Islamic Waqf [property that has been given over by will or as a gift for the public good] throughout the generations and until the Day of Resurrection, no one can renounce it or part of it, or abandon it or part of it. No Arab country nor the aggregate of all Arab countries, and no Arab King or President nor all of them in the aggregate, have that right, nor has that right any organization or the aggregate of all organizations, be they Palestinian or Arab. . . .

Article Twelve. Hamas regards Nationalism (Wataniyya) as part and parcel of the religious faith. Nothing is loftier or deeper in Nationalism than waging Jihad [holy war] against the enemy and confronting him when he sets foot on the land of the Muslims. And this becomes an individual duty binding on every Muslim man and woman; a woman must go out and fight the enemy even without her husband's authorization, and a slave without his masters' permission.

This [principle] does not exist under any other regime, and it is a truth not to be questioned. While other nationalisms consist of material, human and territorial considerations, the nationality of Hamas also carries, in addition to all those, the all important divine factors which lend to it its spirit and life; so much so that it connects with the origin of the spirit and the source of life and raises in the skies of the Homeland the Banner of the Lord, thus inexorably connecting earth with Heaven. . . .

No Solution Except by Jihad

Article Thirteen. [Peace] initiatives, the so-called peaceful solutions, and the international conferences to resolve the Palestinian problem, are all contrary to the beliefs of the Islamic Resistance Movement. For renouncing any part of Palestine means renouncing part of the religion: the nationalism of the Islamic Resistance Movement is part of its faith, the movement educates its members to adhere to its principles and to raise the banner of Allah over their homeland as they fight their Jihad: "Allah is the all-powerful, but most people are not aware. . . ."

Those conferences are no more than a means to appoint the nonbelievers as arbitrators in the lands of Islam. Since when did the Unbelievers do justice to the Believers?

> "And the Jews will not be pleased with thee, nor will the Christians, till thou follow their creed. Say: Lo! the guidance of Allah [himself], is the Guidance. And if you should follow their desires after the knowledge which has come unto thee, then you would have from Allah no protecting friend nor helper." *Sura 2 (the Cow), verse 120.*

There is no solution to the Palestinian problem except by Jihad. The initiatives, proposals and International Conferences are but a waste of time, an exercise in futility. The Palestinian people are too noble to have their futures, their right and their destiny submitted to a vain game. . . .

Article Fourteen. The problem of the liberation of Palestine relates to three circles: the Palestinian, the Arab and the Islamic. Each one of these circles has a role to play in the struggle against Zionism and it has duties to fulfill. It would be an enormous mistake and an abysmal act of ignorance to disregard anyone of these circles. For Palestine is an Islamic land where the First Qibla [the direction Muslims face during worship] and the third holiest site are located. That is also the place whence the Prophet, be Allah's prayer and peace upon him, ascended to Heavens.

> "Glorified be He who carried His servant by night from the Inviolable Place of worship to the Far Distant Place of Worship, the neighborhood whereof we have blessed, that we might show him of our tokens! Lo! He, only He, is the Hearer, the Seer." *Sura XVII (al-Isra'), verse 1.*

In consequence of this state of affairs, the liberation of that land is an individual duty binding on all Muslims everywhere. This is the base on which all Muslims have to regard the problem: this has to be understood by all Muslims. When the problem is dealt with on this basis, where the full potential of the three circles is mobilized, then the current circumstances will change and the day of liberation will come closer. . . .

Article Twenty. Islamic society is one of solidarity. The Messenger of Allah, be Allah's prayer and peace upon him, said:

> What a wonderful tribe were the Ash' aris [members of a school of Islamic theology]! When they were overtaxed, either in their location or during their journeys, they would collect all their possessions and then would divide them equally among themselves.

This is the Islamic spirit which ought to prevail in any Muslim society. A society which confronts a vicious, Nazi-like enemy, who does not differentiate between man and women, elder and young ought to be the first to adorn itself with this Islamic spirit. Our enemy pursues the style of collective punishment of usurping people's countries and properties, of pursuing them into their exiles and places of assembly. It has resorted to breaking bones, opening fire on women and children and the old, with or without reason, and to setting up detention camps where thousands upon thousands are interned in inhuman conditions. In addition, it destroys houses, renders children orphans and issues oppressive judgments against thousands of young people who spend the best years of their youth in the darkness of prisons. The Nazism of the Jews does not skip women and children, it scares everyone. They make war against people's livelihood, plunder their moneys and threaten their honour. In their horrible actions they mistreat people like the most horrendous war criminals. Exiling people from their country is another way of killing them. As we face this misconduct, we have no escape from establishing social solidarity among the people, from confronting the enemy as one solid body, so that if one organ is hurt the rest of the body will respond with alertness and fervor. . . .

Jihad and Imperialism

Article Twenty-two. The enemies have been scheming for a long time, and they have consolidated their schemes, in order to achieve what they have achieved. They took advantage of key-elements in unfolding events, and accumulated a huge and influential material wealth which they put to the service of implementing their dream. This wealth [permitted them to] take over control of the world media such as news agencies, the press, publication houses, broadcasting and the like. [They also used this] wealth to stir revolutions in various parts of the globe in order to fulfill their interests and pick the fruits. They stood behind the French and the Communist Revolutions and behind most of the revolutions we hear about here and there. They also used the money to establish clandestine organizations which are spreading around the world, in order to destroy societies and carry out Zionist interests. Such organizations are: the Free Masons, Rotary Clubs, Lions

Clubs, B'nai B'rith and the like. All of them are destructive spying organizations. They also used the money to take over control of the Imperialist states and made them colonize many countries in order to exploit the wealth of those countries and spread their corruption therein.

As regards local and world wars, it has come to pass and no one objected that they stood behind World War I, so as to wipe out the Islamic Caliphate. They collected material gains and took control of many sources of wealth. They obtained the Balfour Declaration and established the League of Nations in order to rule the world by means of that organization. They also stood behind World War II, where they collected immense benefits from trading with war materials, and prepared for the establishment of their state. They inspired the establishment of the United Nations and the Security Council to replace the League of Nations, in order to rule the world by their intermediary. There was no war that broke out anywhere without their fingerprints on it:

> "As often as they light a fire for war, Allah extinguishes it. Their efforts is for corruption in the land and Allah loves not corrupters." *Sura V (Al-Ma'ida—the Tablespread), verse 64.*

The forces of imperialism in both the Capitalist West and the Communist East support the enemy with all their might, in material and human terms, taking turns between themselves. When Islam appears, all the forces of Unbelief unite to confront it, because the Community of Unbelief is one.

> "Oh ye who believe! Take not for intimates others than your own folk, who would spare no pain to ruin you. Hatred is revealed by [the utterance of] their mouth, but that which their breasts hide is greater. We have made plain for you the revelations if you will understand. . . ." *Sura III (Al-Imran), verse 118.*

It is not in vain that the verse ends with God's saying, "If you will understand. . . ."

Hamas in the Middle East

Article Twenty-six. The Hamas, while it views positively the Palestinian National Movements which do not owe their loyalty to the East or to the West, does not refrain from debating unfolding events regarding the Palestinian problem, on the local and international scenes. These debates are realistic and expose the extent to which [these developments] go along with, or contradict, national interests as viewed from the Islamic vantage point.

Article Twenty-seven. The PLO is among the closest to the Hamas, for it constitutes a father, a brother, a relative, a friend. Can a Muslim turn away from his father, his brother, his relative or his friend? Our homeland is one, our calamity is one, our destiny is one and our enemy is common to both of us. Under the influence of the circumstances which surrounded the founding of the PLO, and the ideological confusion which prevails in the Arab world as a result of the ideological invasion which has swept the Arab world since the rout of the Crusades, and which has been reinforced by Orientalism and the Christian Mission, the PLO has adopted the idea of a Secular State, and so we think of it. Secular thought is diametrically opposed to religious thought. Thought is the basis for positions, for modes of conduct and for resolutions. Therefore, in spite of our appreciation for the PLO and its possible transformation in the future, and despite the fact that we do not denigrate its role in the Arab-Israel conflict, we cannot substitute it for the Islamic nature of Palestine by adopting secular thought. For the Islamic nature of Palestine is part of our religion, and anyone who neglects his religion is bound to lose.

> "And who forsakes the religion of Abraham, save him who befools himself?" *Sura II (Al-Baqra—the Co), verse 130.*

When the PLO adopts Islam as the guideline for life, then we shall become its soldiers, the fuel of its fire which will burn the enemies. And until that happens, and we pray to Allah that it will happen soon, the position of the Hamas towards the PLO is one of a son towards his father, a brother towards his brother, and a relative towards his relative who suffers the other's pain when a thorn hits him, who supports the other in the confrontation with the enemies and who wishes him divine guidance and integrity of conduct. . . .

Article Twenty-eight. The Zionist invasion is a mischievous one. It does not hesitate to take any road, or to pursue all despicable and repulsive means to fulfill its desires. It relies to a great extent, for its meddling and spying activities, on the clandestine organizations which it has established, such as the Free Masons, Rotary Clubs, Lions, and other spying associations. All those secret organizations, some which are overt, act for the interests of Zionism and under its directions, strive to demolish societies, to destroy values, to wreck answerableness, to totter virtues and to wipe out Islam. It stands behind the diffusion of drugs and toxics of all kinds in order to facilitate its control and expansion.

The Arab states surrounding Israel are required to open their borders to the Jihad fighters, the sons of the Arab and Islamic peoples, to enable them to play their role and to join their efforts to those of their brothers among the Muslim Brothers in Palestine.

The other Arab and Islamic states are required, at the very least, to facilitate the movement of the Jihad fighters from and to them. We cannot fail to remind every Muslim that when the Jews occupied Holy Jerusalem in 1967 and stood at the doorstep of the Blessed Aqsa Mosque, they shouted with joy:

"Muhammed is dead, he left daughters behind."

Israel, by virtue of its being Jewish and of having a Jewish population defies Islam and the Muslims. . . .

Article Thirty-one. Hamas is a humane movement, which cares for human rights and is committed to the tolerance inherent in Islam as regards attitudes towards other religions. It is only hostile to those who are hostile towards it, or stand in its way in order to disturb its moves or to frustrate its efforts.

Under the shadow of Islam it is possible for the members of the three religions: Islam, Christianity and Judaism to coexist in safety and security. Safety and security can only prevail under the shadow of Islam, and recent and ancient history is the best witness to that effect. The members of other religions must desist from struggling against Islam over sovereignty in this region. For if they were to gain the upper hand, fighting, torture and uprooting would follow: they would be fed up with each other, to say nothing of members of other religions. The past and the present are full of evidence to that effect.

> "They will not fight you in body safe in fortified villages or from behind wells. Their adversity among themselves is very great. Ye think of them as a whole whereas their hearts are diverse. That is because they are a folk who have no sense." *Sura 59 (al-Hashr, the Exile), verse 14.*

Islam accords his rights to everyone who has rights and averts aggression against the rights of others. The Nazi Zionist practices against our people will not last the lifetime of their invasion, for "States built upon oppression last only one hour, states based upon justice will last until the hour of Resurrection."

> "Allah forbids you not those who warred not against you on account of religion and drove you not out from your houses, that you should show them kindness and deal justly with them. Lo! Allah loves the just dealers." *Sura 60 (Al-Mumtahana), verse 8.*

The Call to Arms

Article Thirty-two. World Zionism and Imperialist forces have been attempting, with smart moves and considered planning, to push the Arab countries, one after another, out of the circle of conflict with Zionism, in order, ultimately, to isolate the Palestinian People. Egypt has already been cast out of the conflict, to a very great extent through the treacherous Camp David Accords, and she has been trying to drag other countries into similar agreements in order to push them out of the circle of conflict.

Hamas is calling upon the Arab and Islamic peoples to act seriously and tirelessly in order to frustrate that dreadful scheme and to make the masses aware of the danger of coping out of the circle of struggle with Zionism. Today it is Palestine and tomorrow it may be another country or other countries. For Zionist scheming has no end, and after Palestine they will covet expansion from the Nile to the Euphrates. Only when they have completed digesting the area on which they will have laid their hand, they will look forward to more expansion, etc. Their scheme has been laid out in the Protocols of the Elders of Zion, and their present [conduct] is the best proof of what is said there.

Leaving the circle of conflict with Israel is a major act of treason and it will bring curse on its perpetrators. . . .

Within the circle of the conflict with world Zionism, the Hamas regards itself the spearhead and the avant-garde. It joins its efforts to all those who are active on the Palestinian scene, but more steps need to be taken by the Arab and Islamic peoples and Islamic associations throughout the Arab and Islamic world in order to make possible the next round with the Jews, the merchants of war. . . .

The greedy have coveted Palestine more than once and they raided it with armies in order to fulfill their covetousness. Multitudes of Crusaders descended on it, carrying their faith with them and waving their Cross. They were able to defeat the Muslims for a long time, and the Muslims were not able to redeem it until they sought the protection of their religious banner; then, they unified their forces, sang the praise of their God and set out for Jihad under the Command of Saladin al-Ayyubi, for the duration of nearly two decades, and then the obvious conquest took place when the Crusaders were defeated and Palestine was liberated.

> "Say (O Muhammed) unto those who disbelieve: ye shall be overcome and gathered unto Hell, an evil resting place." *Sura III (Al-Imran), verse 12.*

This is the only way to liberation, there is no doubt in the testimony of history. That is one of the rules of the universe and one of the laws of existence. Only iron can blunt iron, only the true faith of Islam can vanquish their false and falsified faith. Faith can only be fought by faith. Ultimately, victory is reserved to the truth, and truth is victorious.

The Rising Popularity of Suicide Bombing Among Palestinian Political and Military Factions

By Gal Luft

One important characteristic of the Israeli-Palestinian conflict is the differ-
ence in military resources that each side brings to the battlefield. The Israeli
army is one of the best-equipped and highly trained fighting forces in the
world, but the Palestinian militants only have access to limited and outdated
equipment. In the following article author Gal Luft describes how the poor
results of traditional terror missions at the start of the second Intifada *led*
Palestinian political and military leaders alike to see suicide bombing as an
important tactic.

Related to the increase in suicide bombing, argues Luft, is the fact that
Palestinian militant organizations are ceasing to distinguish between attacks
on settlers, on military targets, and on Israeli civilians behind the pre-1967
boundaries. Because of the increased number of attacks on civilians, many
Israelis want to disengage from the Palestinians by buildings walls and fences
to protect the nation from suicide bombers. This article makes the claim that
these methods of unilateral disengagement will neither solve the problem per-

Gal Luft, "The Palestinian H-Bomb," *Foreign Affairs*, vol. 81, July/August, 2002. Copyright
© 2002 by the Council on Foreign Relations, Inc. Reproduced by permission.

manently nor halt terror attacks in the short term. In the end, Luft argues, more diplomatic methods will be necessary to pursue a lasting peace.

Gal Luft is a former lieutenant colonel in the Israel Defense Forces and the author of The Palestinian Security Forces: Between Police and Army.

N ever in Israel's history, to paraphrase [former prime minister of Great Britain Winston] Churchill, has so much harm been inflicted on so many by so few. Since the onset of the second intifada in late September 2000, dozens of exploding humans—Palestinian H-bombs—have rocked the Jewish state and transformed the lives of its people. As recently as 2001, suicide bombings were seen as a gruesome aberration in the Israeli-Palestinian conflict, an expression of religious fanaticism that most Palestinians rejected. But in recent months a new, unsettling reality has emerged: the acceptance and legitimation of the practice among all Palestinian political and military factions.

Increasingly, Palestinians are coming to see suicide attacks as a strategic weapon, a poor man's "smart bomb" that can miraculously balance Israel's technological prowess and conventional military dominance. Palestinians appear to have decided that, used systematically in the context of a political struggle, suicide bombings give them something no other weapon could: the ability to cause Israel devastating and unprecedented pain. The dream of achieving such strategic parity is more powerful than any pressure to cease and desist. It is therefore unlikely that the strategy will be abandoned, even as its continued use pushes the Middle East ever closer to the abyss.

From Mortars to Martyrs

The Palestinian endorsement of suicide bombings as a legitimate tool of war was not hasty. At the start of the second intifada, the Palestinians' preferred method of fighting was based on the strategy that [the Lebanese terrorist organization] Hezbollah used to drive the Israel Defense Forces (IDF) out of southern Lebanon after 15 years of occupation—a mix of guerrilla tactics such as ambushes, drive-by shootings, and attacks on IDF outposts. It was thought that the "Lebanonization" of the West Bank and the Gaza Strip would cause the Israeli public to view these territories as security liabilities (as they had with southern Lebanon), and to pressure the government to withdraw once more.

Palestinian leader Yasir Arafat's division of labor was clear. His political wing, Fatah, authorized its paramilitary units, spearheaded by the Tanzim militias along with segments of the security services of the Palestinian Authority (PA), to carry out a guerrilla campaign against Israeli settlements and military targets in the West Bank and Gaza. The militant groups Hamas and Islamic Jihad, meanwhile, were given the liberty to carry out attacks against civilian targets inside Israel.

From the Palestinian perspective, however, the results of the guerrilla campaign in the first year were poor, especially considering the duration of the fighting and the volume of fire. Palestinian forces launched more than 1,500 shooting attacks on Israeli vehicles in the territories but killed 75 people. They attacked IDF outposts more than 6,000 times but killed only 20 soldiers. They fired more than 300 antitank grenades at Israeli targets but failed to kill anyone. To demoralize the settlers, the Palestinians launched more than 500 mortar and rocket attacks at Jewish communities in the territories and, at times, inside Israel, but the artillery proved to be primitive and inaccurate, and only one Israeli was killed.

Israel's response to the guerrilla campaign, moreover, was decisive. Using good intelligence, the Israeli security services targeted individual Palestinian militants and destroyed most of the PA's military infrastructure. Israeli soldiers also moved back into "Area A," the territory that had been turned over as a result of the Oslo peace negotiations to exclusive Palestinian control, to raze suspected mortar activity sites. At first these incursions met with international rebuke, even from the United States. Secretary of State Colin Powell, for example, denounced the first foray into Gaza in April 2001 as "excessive and disproportionate." But over time the temporary incursions became such a common practice that the international community stopped paying attention. Stung by the lack of progress in the struggle, at the end of 2001 Arafat tried a final gambit, attempting to smuggle in a cache of Iranian weapons on board the *Karine-A*. But Israeli naval commandos seized the ship and turned his ploy into a shameful diplomatic disaster. Thus ended Palestinian emulation of the "Hezbollah model."

Unlike the guerrilla strategy, meanwhile, the terror campaign carried out by Hamas and Islamic Jihad was showing results. The Islamic movements managed to kill or maim more Israelis in 350 stabbings, shootings, and bombings inside Israel than the mainstream Palestinian organizations had in more than 8,000 armed attacks in the West Bank and Gaza. The strongest impact came from 39 suicide attacks that killed 70 Israelis and wounded more than 1,000 others. If one compares this bloodshed with the limited damage caused by the 39 Scud missiles [former Iraqi president] Saddam Hussein launched at Israel in 1991—74 fatalities, most of them caused by heart attacks—it is not hard to understand why the new methods caused such intoxication.

Palestinians are fully aware of what they have suffered at the hands of the Israeli military in response to the terror campaign, but most view it as a great success nevertheless. They derive comfort and satisfaction from the fact that the Jews are also suffering. The Palestinians view the campaign's greatest achievement as not just the killing of so many Israelis but the decline of Israel's economy, the destruction of its tourism industry, and the demoralization of its people. According to a mid-May [2002] poll, two-thirds of Palestinians say that the second intifada's violence has achieved more for them than did the previous years of negotiations.

Legitimizing Terror

Before the outbreak of the second intifada, Palestinians distinguished among attacks on settlers, on Israeli military targets, and on civilians inside Israel. Now, however, those distinctions are disappearing. Although after the Israeli incursions [in the] spring [of 2002] support for attacks against civilians inside Israel dropped 6 points to 52 percent, opposition to arresting those carrying out such attacks rose 10 points to 86 percent—a figure close to the 89 percent and 92 percent support for attacks on Israeli settlers and soldiers in the territories, respectively.

In the post-9/11 [September 11, 2001, World Trade Center terrorist attacks] era, however, when deliberate attacks against innocent civilians are anathema to most people, embracing terrorism as a strategy has required the Palestinians to persuade themselves, and others, that what they are doing is legitimate. They have therefore created what they see as a moral equivalence between Israel's harm to the Palestinian civilian population and Palestinian attacks against Israeli civilians, including children.

They have also developed a creative interpretation of what terrorism is, one that stresses ends rather than means. Thus, in December 2001, more than 94 percent of Palestinians told pollsters that they viewed Israeli incursions into Area A as acts of terror, while 82 percent refused to characterize the killing of 21 Israeli youths outside a Tel Aviv disco six months earlier that way. And 94 percent reported that they would characterize a hypothetical Israeli use of chemical or biological weapons against Palestinians as terrorism, whereas only 26 percent would say the same about Palestinian use of those weapons against Israel. Interestingly, the new definition extends beyond the conflict with Israel. Only 41 percent of Palestinians, for example, viewed the September 11 attacks as terrorism, and only 46 percent saw the Lockerbie bombing [of Pan Am flight 103 in 1988] that way.

The more enchanted Palestinians have become with the achievements of their "martyrs," the more Fatah has found itself under pressure to adopt the suicide weapon. [In 2001], fearing a loss of popular support if the "street" perceived the Islamists' methods as more effective than Fatah's tack, Fatah leaders decided they had to follow suit.

The part of Arafat that wanted to show solidarity with the United States and that was determined to avoid any association with terror against civilians, in other words, succumbed to the anti-Israel rage and political calculations of his lieutenants and the members of what Palestinian pollster Khalil Shikaki has called the "young guard" of Palestinian nationalism.

Fatah's official espousal of "martyrdom" operations took place on November 29, 2001, when two terrorists blew themselves up together on a bus near the Israeli city of Hadera. One, Mustafa Abu Srieh, was from Islamic Jihad; the other, Abdel Karim Abu Nafa, served with the Palestinian police in Jericho. But the bond of blood with the Islamists did not last long, and soon Fatah's al Aqsa Martyrs Brigades and the Islamists found themselves engaged in a diabolical contest over which group could perfect the use of the suicide weapon and be viewed as most valuable to the war effort. Al Aqsa has capitalized on the Islamists' opposition to the participation of women and established squads of willing female suicide bombers named after Wafa Idris, the Palestinian woman who blew up herself and an Israeli man in Jerusalem in January. Islamic Jihad, for its part, has recruited children as young as 13 for suicide missions.

Both Islamists and secular Palestinians have come to see suicide bombing as a weapon against which Israel has no comprehensive defense. To counter the Iraqi Scuds, Israel developed and deployed the Arrow, a $2 billion ballistic missile defense system. Against Palestinian H-bombs, Israel can at best build a fence. The suicide bombers are smarter than Scuds, and Palestinians know that even though in Israel today there are more security guards than teachers or doctors, the bomber will always get through.

No Military Solution

If history is any guide, Israel's military campaign to eradicate the phenomenon of suicide bombing is unlikely to succeed. Other nations that have faced opponents willing to die have learned the hard way that, short of complete annihilation of the enemy, no military solution will solve the problem.

But the Israeli authorities are deeply reluctant to accept this reality. Israeli society seeks absolute security and adheres to the notion that military power can resolve almost any security problem. If the Palestinians put their faith in Allah, Israelis put theirs in a tank. Whether consciously or not, their belief in the utility of force—evident in the popular "Let the IDF Win" campaign, which advocated a freer hand for the army—reflects a strategic choice to militarize the conflict rather than politicize it. The IDF's senior leaders repeatedly claim that the smart application of military force can create a new reality on the ground that, in turn, will allow the government to negotiate political agreements under more favorable terms.

It is true that when the IDF was finally allowed to "win," Israel achieved impressive tactical results. Operation Defensive Shield [in April 2002] eliminated an entire echelon of terrorist leaders in the West Bank, crippled the PA's financial and operational infrastructure, and reduced PA arsenals. But as at other times in its history, Israel failed to convert its tactical achievements into strategic gains. Its intensive use of military instruments earned it international condemnation, further radicalized Palestinian society, and created an environment of anger conducive to more terrorist activities. By May, unsurprisingly, the suicide bombings had started again.

IDF simulations before the second intifada had predicted that a military reentry into major Palestinian cities would lead to hundreds of Israeli casualties. In fact, however, the incursions into territories under Palestinian control proved to be almost painless. Following the assassination of Israel's tourism minister, Rehavam Ze'evi, in October 2001, the IDF launched a broad assault on the PA, entering all six major West Bank cities. Palestinian resistance was negligible, and only six Israeli soldiers were wounded. Operation Defensive Shield, the second big incursion into Area A, also met relatively weak resistance. Aside from the struggle in the Jenin refugee camp, in which 23 Israeli soldiers were killed, Israeli forces conquered six Palestinian cities and dozens of smaller towns and villages while suffering only three fatalities.

The IDF has interpreted the Palestinian lack of resistance in the cities as a sign of weakness rather than a strategic choice. Israelis view with disdain the Palestinian "victory" celebrations after each incursion comes to an end. They are puzzled by the fact that their enemy fires more bullets into the air than at Israeli troops. What Israel fails to comprehend is the paradigm by which the Palestinians are choosing to conduct their war.

Acknowledging their perpetual conventional inferiority, Arafat's people feel no need to demonstrate strong resistance to Israeli forces. They simply wait for the storm to pass while preparing another batch of "martyrs." Families of suicide bombers now receive more than double the financial compensation than do the families of those killed by other means. Nurturing an ethos of heroism fundamentally opposed to that of the Israelis, the Palestinian war of liberation has elevated the suicide bomber to the highest throne of courage and devotion to the national cause.

Israelis' misunderstanding of the new Palestinian way of war may come back to haunt them. Their perception of their enemy's weakness is likely to embolden them and encourage more broad punitive operations in response to future attacks. But Israel's military responses will eventually exhaust themselves, whereas the Palestinians will still have legions of willing "martyrs."

In fact, despite defiant Israeli rhetoric insisting that there will be no surrender to terrorism, one can already see the opposite happening. Israelis are willing to pay an increasingly high economic and diplomatic price for increasingly short periods of calm. As a result, more and more people support panaceas such as unilateral separation—the building of walls, fences, and buffer zones to protect Israel's population centers from Palestinian wrath.

Unilateral separation would no doubt make the infiltration of suicide bombers into Israel more difficult, but it would also increase their prestige in the eyes of many in the region. The bombers would be viewed, correctly, as the catalyst that drove the Israelis out of an occupied territory yet again, and the years of agony Palestinians have endured would be sweetened by a genuine sense of victory. Israel's wall policy, perceived as withdrawal, would reassure the Palestinians that war succeeded where diplomacy failed.

As currently conceived, moreover, walling off the territories would not do much to reduce Palestinian grievances. No matter how long the fence, for example, dozens of Jewish settlements scattered on the hills of the West Bank would necessarily remain beyond it. Two-thirds of Israelis, according to recent polls, support the removal of such isolated and indefensible settlements to make the separation more feasible. But despite such views, Israeli Prime Minister Ariel Sharon has reiterated his refusal to dismantle a single settlement. "The fate of Netzarim is the fate of Tel Aviv," he said recently, referring to the tiny, isolated, and fortified Gaza Strip settlement that has been the target of repeated Palestinian attacks.

Defusing the Bomb

Israel finds itself, therefore, at a crucial turning point in its history, but one from which no path seems particularly attractive. It must find some way of defending itself against an enemy so eager to inflict pain that it is willing to bring suffering and death on itself in the process. Retaliation is unlikely to work, but retreat is likely only to bring more of the same.

If there is any way out of this dilemma, it may lie in convincing the Palestinian public that its constructive goals can be achieved only by relinquishing its destructive strategy. Israel should therefore embark on a policy that rewards the Palestinians for genuinely fighting terrorism and avoid any policy that feeds the perception that terrorism works.

The rewards will have to be tangible and meaningful. Israel could, for example, offer the PA the removal of a number of small hilltop settlements in exchange for a period of non-belligerency and unequivocal renunciation of suicide bombing. This cooling-off period could then set the stage for renewed talks on a final-status agreement. Such an approach would indicate to the Palestinian population that Israel is serious about peace and ready to pay the necessary price for it, not only in words but in deeds. Most important, showing that Israel is prepared to confront and rein in its own radical rejectionists would put the onus on the Palestinian leadership to do the same.

Before this intifada, a large majority of Palestinians opposed attacks against civilians inside Israel. They hoped to achieve their aspirations for independence without resort to terror. Figuring out how to make that happen is not only the right thing to do, but it is also the best way to ensure Israel's security. Unless that hope can be revived, the fate of Tel Aviv could indeed become that of Netzarim—which would be a tragedy for all.

Israel Does Not Accept Responsibility for Its Role in the Present Conflict

By Hasan Abdel Rahman

One of the major problems fueling the fire of the current conflict, according to Hasan Abdel Rahman, the chief Palestinian representative in the United States, is that the Israelis have been unwilling to take responsibility for their role as aggressors throughout the history of the present conflict. In this speech to the Commonwealth Club on May 16, 2002, Rahman traces this history of blind aggression, including the failures at Oslo and Camp David, in an attempt to show how the conflict will continue until the Israelis acknowledge their behavior up to the present and accept the right of the Palestinians to have their own legitimate and complete state, sharing a border as equals. The Commonwealth Club, founded in 1903, is the oldest and largest public affairs forum in the United States and is based in San Francisco.

Twenty-five years ago [1977], President Jimmy Carter invited me to attend a reception hosted by Kurt Waldheim, then secretary general of the United Nations. The organized American-Jewish community protested. As I was leaving the building of the UN, the press, which was not allowed into the reception, asked President Carter, "Did you shake the hand of the representative of the PLO?" President Carter said, "I don't remember," because it was very costly then for the president of the United States to shake hands with a Palestinian representative. In 1987, we reminisced on this occasion. President Carter said that if he had to do it again he would have done it differently. He realized that denial only generates denial, and recognition generates recognition.

The Palestinian-Israeli conflict is probably the most covered and most written-about conflict in human history—yet the least understood conflict. From our point of view, we are not yet able to tell our story. Others narrate our story, and that's why I appreciate this opportunity to share with you our side of this story.

Many people, when they want to describe this conflict, say it is a religious conflict between Muslims and Jews. Or an issue of violence and terrorism: "Those Palestinians are just naturally like that; they're terrorists. And you cannot coexist with terrorists." Many people do not want to acknowledge that this conflict is about national rights, a conflict between the national movement of the Jewish people and the national movement of the Palestinian people. The Jewish people felt persecuted in Europe and searched for a homeland to solve their problem—a European problem, not a Middle Eastern problem, because we did not persecute Jews for being Jews. Never. The best periods in the history of the Jewish people were the thousands of years when they coexisted with Muslims in the south of Spain or north of Africa or in the cities of Cairo, Baghdad, Damascus. They lived as part of this mosaic of the Middle East. If we are proud of our legacy, it is that legacy of coexistence and tolerance among the three monotheistic faiths in our region: Christianity, Judaism and Islam.

Since 1897, when the World Zionist Movement decided to establish a Jewish state in Palestine, we have had conflict. The conflict is not 1,000 or 2,000 or even 200 years old. This is a modern conflict. It is the nationalism of the Jewish people imposed against the nationalism of the Palestinian people in Palestine. The Jews paid a very heavy price in Europe at the hands of the Nazis, the anti-Semites in Russia, Ukraine, Eastern Europe. But we paid the price for the persecution of the Jews; the Jewish problem was solved at our expense. In 1948, when Israel was created, half of the Palestinian people became homeless; they were expelled or left. Those are the Palestinians who today live as refugees in Lebanon, Syria, Jordan, in the refugee camps of Jenin, Haish and other cities of Gaza and in what is left of Palestine. My generation of Palestinians, then four or five years old, became stateless. The West Bank became Jordanian. Gaza came under Egyptian administration. We grew up not being able to identify ourselves as Palestinians. We witnessed the suffering of our people in refugee camps, not able to exercise their right to self-determination and live as free people. As people dealt us an injustice, we decided that we needed to rise up and restore independence and sovereignty to our people. We fought Israel because the creation of Israel, through gathering Jews from all over the world into Palestine, was the main reason for the situation we found ourselves in.

Fighting for Recognition

We cannot ignore this part of history. Many would like to see this conflict as if it started two months ago, or three months ago, or 18 months ago—it started 54 years ago [in 1948]. It will not be settled unless justice is restored. We do not ask for absolute justice; we ask for minimum justice. After years of confrontation with Israel and World Zionism, we came to a conclusion. I was one of the Palestinians who in 1975 called for the recognition of the state of Israel within 1967 boundaries. Many Palestinians like myself—then a minority—decided this conflict could not be a zero-sum game, neither total justice for us nor total victory for Israel. This conflict cannot be solved militarily; it has to be solved politically, through the establishment of two states. We opted to partition Palestine.

This 1975 proposal was not accepted by the Israelis, although our national council in 1974 called for the establishment of a Palestinian national authority on the Palestinian territories from which Israel would withdraw. Prime Minister of Israel Golda Meir said, "Who are those Palestinians? They never existed. There were no Palestinians here." We had to fight in order to tell the Israelis, "Yes, we do exist." The price was very costly for both Israel and for us. We fought each other until 1992, when a courageous leader in Israel, Yitzhak Rabin, and Yasser Arafat, with help of the U.S., came to an agreement based on the principle of partitioning historic Palestine between the Palestinian people and Israel and mutual recognition between the PLO and the state of Israel. We devised the Oslo process that would lead us to permanent peace.

The Failure at Oslo

The plan to achieve this would create a Palestinian national authority on the West Bank and Gaza, and we would engage in two parallel steps. One was to build institutions of the Palestinian national authority while Israel phased out its presence in the West Bank and Gaza. Through incremental steps, Israel would transfer power in areas of public administration to Palestinian authorities, and it would withdraw its troops, dismantle the civil administration the occupation established and withdraw the Israeli military government. That was the agreement, and at the conclusion of four years, we would negotiate with Israel the "Final Status Issues": Jerusalem, the refugees, the settlements, the water, the borders and security.

Instead of phasing out its military presence in the West Bank and Gaza, by the end of 2000, we had 100,000 more Jewish settlers in the West Bank and Gaza. We saw an invasion by Jewish settlers, under the protection and with the support of the Israeli government. That is in contradiction with the spirit and the letter of the Oslo agreement. With each new settlement there were more Israeli soldiers. Those settlers— mainly from Brooklyn, New York and Moscow—were armed and would take land from Palestinian peasants. The Israeli soldiers were also armed. The Palestinians started accusing the Palestinian Authority of being collaborators with Israel because we tolerated the presence of the Israeli army and continued to negotiate with Israel. We were hoping that ultimately we would reach an agreement.

When we raised the issue of the intensification of settlement in the West Bank to the American government, President [Bill] Clinton would say, "Focus on the big issue. We do not want to really invest our energies on those little issues such as the behavior of the Israeli army in the territories or the presence of Jewish settlers. You will have an agreement that will give you a state of your own and all those issues will be solved." For me, as a negotiator across the table from the Israeli delegation, that was okay. But the average Palestinian citizen only sees from Israel not the niceties of [Acting Foreign Minister] Shlomo Ben-Ami and [Minister of Regional Cooperation] Shimon Peres but the gun of the Israeli soldier and the Israeli settler. For him, relations with Israel were oppression and occupation. So-called dividends of the peace process were not felt by the average Palestinian. There was a disconnection between the agreements that we were signing with Israel on the table and what was happening on the ground.

The Failure at Camp David

We reached Camp David in 2000, hoping for an agreement. Pro-Israeli apologists in the U.S. say the Palestinians rejected a very generous offer by [Prime Minister Ehud] Barak. At Camp David, the Israelis never made a formal offer to us. They floated ideas through the American delegation. On refugees, the Israeli chief of the committee negotiating with us, Elyakim Rubinstein, said in his opening statement, "Israel bears no responsibility, legal or moral, on the issue of the Palestinian refugees." We said, "Are you serious? Those people came from 385 towns that were demolished by Israel, and your historians and archives indicate that 80 percent of them were driven out by the paramilitary organizations of Israel. Those who were from Lod and Ramle, two cities, were driven out by none other than Yitzhak Rabin, who was a colonel in the Israeli army then."

This is history. This happened in the lifetime of those people who were negotiating at the table. Some were children then and were driven out with their families. How can you claim that you do not have legal or moral responsibility? We have a problem here, because the refugee issue is an integral part of the conflict between the Palestinians and the Israelis. And [the] Israelis, more than anybody else, should not say this, because [they] are claiming reparations for the Jews from Europe, even today. We support [them] because no one should be denied their inalienable right to their private property. There are many homes that were built by Palestinians in which today Jews are living. [The Jews] have an organization called the Department for Absentee Landlords. [They] rent those properties to [their] citizens. Those properties are ours; we have our deeds with us. An Israeli will tell you, "The Palestinians want to bring 5 million Palestinians to occupy Israel and to destroy Israel from within." That is not the case. We want a fair solution for the refugee problem that will affect neither the character nor the security of the state of Israel and that is consistent with the two-state solution.

With the issue of territories, we said, "We formally renounce our right to sovereignty in 78 percent that today is the state of Israel. We accept only 22 percent of historic Palestine, the West Bank and Gaza." Mr. Barak said, "I cannot give you the whole West Bank and Gaza. I have to keep the Jewish settlements that were built there." "But those Jewish settlements were built there illegally." "No, I cannot remove them," Mr. Barak said.

Three blocks of settlements will dissect the West Bank into three separate regions and render the West Bank a non-state. Also, Israel wanted control over borders with Jordan to the east, and control over the two major water aquifers in the north and the south of the West Bank. They want the water, the space, the air space, the borders with Jordan, and they will give us three pieces of territory that will constitute 15 percent of what was ours. That is a generous offer in the eyes of many Israelis.

The Jerusalem Issue

On the issues of Jerusalem, we said, "We accept your control over the Wailing Wall; that's the holy place for the Jews. Why do you want to go into the mosque?" They said, "Because the temple was under the mosque." "Maybe the temple was under the mosque, but there's no temple anymore, so your relationship with the temple is a memory, an emotion. For us there is a mosque that has been there for 1,400 years continuously in which the Muslim world worships. It is an important religious place. Have your memory linked to this place, but there's a concrete place for you where you will worship. For us there is the mosque, and we will have control of it." They said, "No, you will have control over the ground; we will have control under the ground." "Let's assume we have an earthquake tomorrow and the mosque is destroyed. Who has the right to issue a permit if you have the sovereignty under the ground and we have it over the ground?" . . .

We did not reach an agreement, but that did not stop the negotiations with Israel. We continued to negotiate even after Camp David, until September 28, when Mr. [Ariel] Sharon decided to return to Israeli politics. The best show that he could make was to go to Al-Haram Sharif, to Al-Aqsa Mosque and, accompanied by 2,000 armed Israeli citizens, declare that he was there to assert Jewish sovereignty over this Muslim holy place. That was provocation. Mr. Barak was the prime minister. We told the Americans, "Don't let Sharon go to Al-Haram Sharif. If he goes there and says, 'I want to assert Jewish sovereignty over this place,' he is provoking not only the Palestinian Muslims, but Muslims all over the world. With Israel, if we discuss the issue of Jerusalem we will be discussing political sovereignty, but if it is a Jewish-Islamic thing, it is a religious conflict." Mr. Barak did not listen to us. Mr. Clinton did not listen to us. And Mr. Sharon went there.

The Al-Aqsa *Intifada*

The day he arrived at Al-Haram Sharif there were protests by the Palestinians. The next morning eight Palestinians were killed in peaceful protest by the Israeli army. The next day the Palestinians wanted to bury their dead from the day before; the Israeli army fired at them and killed 14 more; 300 were wounded. On the third day 15 Palestinians were killed, also in peaceful demonstrations before any shot was fired at the Israelis. By day four we had 49 Palestinians killed and 1,000 wounded. After that we could not control our people. They said to the authorities, "If you don't want to protect us, if your partners in peace are shooting at us and killing our people, we have to defend ourselves."

Since September 28, we've had 3,000 Palestinians killed; 400 are children under the age of 16. Eighty of them were children killed on their way to school with their backpacks on their backs. We've had 600 homes demolished by Israel, hundreds of acres of crops destroyed. Every institution that belongs to the Palestinian authorities—every electricity facility, every telephone pole—was destroyed by Israel. Israel waged a war against everything that the Palestinian society has. Our losses are almost, in terms of the public and private sector, $8 billion. Today the Israeli army is encircling every single city and town of the West Bank. Palestinians are not allowed to move from one area to the other. Sixty percent are unemployed, 60 percent cannot provide food for their children. Then Israel asks why there is violence. This

THE CAUSES OF CONFLICT 101

occupation after 35 years is a system of violence where you keep a whole nation under control, under curfew.

I don't believe there is any people today who lives under foreign military occupation except the Palestinian people. Building of settlements, illegal colonies, in the Palestinian territories has continued. Since [2001], 35 new settlements have been built. Today, in the West Bank and Gaza, there are 60,000 Israeli soldiers and thousands of tanks. In the refugee camp in Jenin, Israel used helicopters to attack civilians. It demolished homes. Look at the Human Rights Watch report, the report by Amnesty International, the report of the United Nations. I would have expected the Jewish community to be outraged when crimes that were committed against them were committed by their children today against the Palestinians. This is not in the interest of Israel. It is not the way to build confidence between the two peoples.

Attacks on Civilians

We continue to declare publicly that we condemn and are appalled by attacks by Palestinians against Jewish civilians. Not only because of what it does to Israel, but also because of what it does to our society. I cannot morally or legally or politically tolerate suicide bombing. But it is not enough to condemn it. You have to understand the causes. Look at the conditions created by the Israeli military presence in the Palestinian territories that turn the average Palestinian citizen into a human being who does not distinguish between life and death. The occupation created a culture of violence in the Palestinian territories.

We are a peaceful society. I challenge anyone to look at the history of the West Bank before Israel's occupation: If we had two homicides a year in the whole territory, that was too many. Today a Palestinian is killed and it is treated as numbers: five Palestinians killed today—10, 13, 14, terrorists, refugees. We have become dehumanized and depersonalized. What you see in the American media is "Ten Palestinian fighters killed," "Ten Palestinian terrorists killed." It is a deliberate dehumanization of the Palestinian. That is not the way to establish peace.

Israel will live there forever and we will live there forever. If they kick us out to Jordan or to Lebanon, we will always be on the borders of Israel. We cannot forget our homeland. The principle of partition and coexistence is the only option. Denial of the existence of those crimes does not help that. America has to address it before anybody else, because America provides Israel with $3 billion every year in military and economic aid. Israel has received $100 billion from the United States since 1979. Israel is protected by the U.S. at the United Nations. The . . . U.S. voted to sponsor a solution at the Security Council calling for an investigation of what happened in Jenin. Israel said,

"We do not have anything to hide." The next day they said, "We do not want to because we are afraid that those investigations will lead to war crime trials of the Israeli soldiers." This kind of behavior creates chaos in the international political system.

If Israel is allowed to defy international resolutions and the Security Council resolutions, what makes it unacceptable for other states also to defy international resolutions? For the Arab world, which sees that Palestinians are being killed by planes provided by the U.S., it cannot be hidden anymore. When they see those pictures on their networks, they are provoked.

A Two-State Solution

There is only one solution: for the two people to coexist next to each other in two separate states. The U.S. and the world community are of this opinion. But the decision made by the Likud Party of Mr. Sharon is sending the wrong message to the Palestinians. Denial and negation generate denial and negation. If you negate the right of the Palestinians to their own state, Palestinians are going to negate the right of Israel to exist. If there is recognition of the right of the Palestinian state there will be recognition of the right of Israel to exist.

There is a window of opportunity. There are efforts underway. The Arab world made a proposal in Beirut in which they established the foundations of a permanent peace between Israel and the Palestinians and the rest of the Arab world. Either we have Israel withdraw from all the territories—and the Arab world will recognize Israel and establish normal diplomatic relations with it—or the Middle East will be plunged into a conflict that will have serious ramifications for not only the Israelis, Palestinians and Arabs, but also for the United States and the world. The region is extremely important for the world economy. I hope the efforts of the U.S. administration and wisdom of the peace camp in Israel, together with ours, who are committed to a permanent peace in our region, based on recognition between the two sides, based on two states, will prevail. We owe it to our children, to the Israeli children and to this and future generations of both peoples.

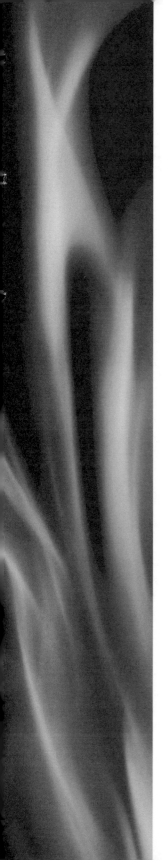

CHAPTER 3

The Paths to Peace

Jerusalem Is a Central Component of Any Lasting Peace

By Rashid Khalidi

The city of Jerusalem is an important holy place for three of the world's largest religions, housing holy sites for Christians, Muslims, and Jews alike. In order for a peaceful resolution to the Israeli-Palestinian conflict, argues Rashid Khalidi, director of the Center for International Studies at the University of Chicago, there are three key issues that must be resolved regarding Jerusalem. First, the resolution must produce a system so that Palestinians and Israelis can share the city in an equal and open manner. Second, it must allow Jerusalem to operate as the capital of both the Israeli and the Palestinian states. And third, it must allow people of all religions to have open access to the many important holy sites throughout the city.

The first step in the process, Khalidi argues in this article from the Journal of Palestine Studies, *is to erase the idea that Jerusalem is only important to Israeli Jews, a misconception that he claims was fostered during the Bill Clinton administration. Once this error is corrected, Israelis and Palestinians can move on to the more important aspects of the Jerusalem issue, such as establishing a system for an open city and coming up with strategies for security and shared sovereignty. Once these strategies are in place, the possibility of a lasting peace will be one step nearer.*

M ore than any other issue of the Palestinian-Israeli conflict, Jerusalem has deep resonance for all the parties. Certainly, there will be no end to the Palestinian-Israeli conflict, no Arab-Israeli rec-

Rashid Khalidi, "The Centrality of Jerusalem to an End of Conflict Agreement," *Journal of Palestine Studies*, vol. 30, Spring 2001, p. 82. Copyright © 2001 by Institute for Palestine Studies. Reproduced by permission.

onciliation, and no normalization of the situation of Israel in the region without a lasting solution for Jerusalem. For a solution to be seen by all parties as satisfying, it must accomplish three things: it must allow Palestinians and Israelis to share the city equitably; it must allow Jerusalem to be the capital of both Palestine and Israel; and it must allow people of all faiths to have free and unimpeded access to Jerusalem.

During the Clinton administration, however, a line of argument prevailed that Jerusalem is really important to only one religious tradition, the Jewish one; and that it is really important to only one people, the Israelis. This intolerant and ignorant thesis is essentially aimed at keeping treatment of the Jerusalem issue in U.S. policy where it has been for the past eight years—hostage to the assumption that the only important question regarding Jerusalem is what Israel will accept.

Indeed, this assumption has extended to all issues of the conflict. For the last eight years [since 1993], the ceiling of the negotiations brokered by the United States has been what American policymakers—often mistakenly—claimed to be the outer limits of what Israel would accept. Thus, they argued that Israel would never negotiate with the PLO, would never accept the idea of a Palestinian state, would never withdraw from Lebanon, would never accept a complete withdrawal from the Golan Heights, and would never accept Palestinian sovereignty over parts of East Jerusalem. Over time, of course, the past three Israeli governments—those of Yitzhak Rabin, Benjamin Netanyahu, and Ehud Barak—came to accept the possibility, and in some cases the reality, of all of these options that American "experts" claimed were unthinkable for Israel. The converse of the American policy assumption that all that matters is what Israel will accept is the policy's total disregard for what the Arab parties could accept.

Jerusalem as Capital of Two States

Peace in the Middle East does not have to be made—as some appear to believe—between Israel's Likud and Labor parties. It has to be made between Palestinians and Israelis, and between Arabs and Israelis, and it must take into account the concerns of Muslims, Christians, and Jews everywhere. Indeed, where Jerusalem is involved, the need to consider the concerns of a broad range of constituencies is more urgent than with any other issue in the Arab-Israeli conflict, because of Jerusalem's profound resonance for so many people.

For confirmation of how important Jerusalem is to peace in the Middle East, one has only to look at events since September 2000. The new Palestinian intifada, named for the al-Aqsa Mosque in Jerusalem, exploded following Ariel Sharon's provocative visit to affirm Israeli sovereignty over the third holiest site in Islam and the killing of seven unarmed Palestinian protestors the following day. Sharon's first act after winning the 6 February 2001 election for prime minister was to visit the Western Wall plaza and proclaim Israeli sovereignty over occupied Arab East Jerusalem. We have seen since the Camp David negotiations of July 2000 how central Jerusalem can be to conflict in the Middle East. But it is also essential to ask how it can be central to ending the conflict.

One issue insufficiently stressed by those laying the groundwork for an agreement is the absolute centrality of a mutually satisfying resolution on Jerusalem to achieving an end considered extremely important by Israel's supporters: this is acceptance of Israel in the Middle East and normalization of its relations with its neighbors. The desire for this objective is great among many in Israel (although the Israeli prime minister-elect and some of his supporters do not appear to share it). It was also apparent in Prime Minister Barak's quest in negotiations as of July 2000 for an agreement on a final end to the conflict with the Palestinians.

In view of this desire, it would be advantageous to all concerned for the Palestinians and the other Arab parties, and also the United States, to put forward proposals whereby Israel would obtain recognition of Jerusalem as its capital in exchange for Israeli recognition of Jerusalem as the capital of Palestine, with all that acceptance entails. What Israelis perceive as a major concession on their part (and Arabs perceive as no more than implementation of UN Security Council resolutions and international law) can thus be shown to be something of great benefit both to Israelis and to the Palestinians and other Arabs.

The converse must be mentioned. If Israel does not recognize Jerusalem as the capital of Palestine, with all that entails, Jerusalem will never be recognized as the capital of Israel in the Arab world, the Muslim world, and in many, perhaps most, other parts of the world, which have withheld such recognition for the past fifty-two years.

It should be emphasized, however, that this is not self-evident. It therefore is necessary for the Palestinians, the Arab parties, and U.S. policymakers and diplomats to stress the positive aspect of this trade-off, which is that the only way to achieve universal recognition and acceptance of Jerusalem as the capital of Israel, and of Israeli sovereignty over part of the city, is for Israel to recognize Jerusalem as the capital of Palestine and to recognize Palestinian sovereignty over occupied Arab East Jerusalem.

What are the most important elements regarding Jerusalem in a potential end of conflict agreement? First is unimpeded access to Jerusalem for Palestinians, for Muslims and Christians from other Arab countries, and for Muslims from other countries. This can only mean access under Palestinian control. Second is a satisfactory and mutually acceptable regime for control over and security in the Muslim, Christian, and Jewish holy places in Jerusalem. This will require significant changes in the status quo. And third is Palestinian sovereignty over Arab East Jerusalem (the largest Arab city in the West Bank), as a single unit, with contiguity of the city's Arab neighborhoods and open road connections with adjacent Palestinian regions of the West Bank to the north, south, and east.

Each of these three points must be seen not as Palestinian desiderata [essential desires] (which they are), but as prerequisites for the acceptance of Israel as a normal part of the Middle East region. Do Israelis seriously assume that other Arabs and Muslims will accept that all details of the life of Palestinian residents of Jerusalem, from control over open space, to sewage, to freedom of movement, should be permanently governed solely by the requirements of the comfort and security of Israeli residents of the city? Do they seriously assume that Arabs and Muslims will accept permanently a situation where Palestinians, as well as Muslim or Christian pilgrims from the Arab countries, should have to submit to the humiliations of Israeli security controls before being allowed to worship in Jerusalem? How would they feel if Jews were to be subjected to similar humiliations before they were allowed to worship there?

Only if one begins from the invidious premise that Jerusalem is important primarily to Israelis, and is more precious to Jews than to adherents of any other faith, can such assumptions be justified. It is up to the Palestinians, the Arabs, and to American policymakers and diplomats to show Israelis and their influential supporters in the United States that it is as advantageous to Israel as to other parties to accept free, unimpeded access for Palestinians and other Arabs and Muslims to Jerusalem, a satisfactory security and control regime for all of Jerusalem's holy places, and Palestinian sovereignty over Arab East Jerusalem. Until now, however, Palestinians largely have failed to articulate a vision embodying this reality either in the United States or in Israel. Doing so is an essential part of laying the groundwork for a just and lasting solution to the conflict.

A starting point for such a vision can be the three points mentioned above. We can look at each of these points in more detail. For example, the question of access to Jerusalem involves three important considerations. The first relates to Jerusalem as the center of life for the West Bank and Gaza Strip, given its importance as a center of education; of professional, medical, and consular services; and of wholesale and retail trade, all of which require free and unimpeded access to the city for the 3 million Palestinians of the West Bank and Gaza Strip, access that has been denied to them since the start of the peace process in 1991.

The second involves Jerusalem's centrality as a communications node for the entire West Bank, as the sole linkage point for the road network running along the north-south ridge line between the Nablus and Ramallah areas to the north and the Hebron and Bethlehem areas to the south. This necessitates unimpeded road access for Palestinians to and through the city, which they have not had for a decade. And finally, it is a destination for Christian and Muslim worshippers and pilgrims from throughout Palestine. Those of the West Bank and Gaza Strip have been denied this opportunity since Israel imposed on them the "closure" of Jerusalem in 1991.

All of these considerations require that Arab East Jerusalem function as a single unit with contiguity between its various Arab neighborhoods and that there be unimpeded road connections to the rest of the West Bank. This could be done in the context of the entirety of Jerusalem remaining a single open city, with a single joint municipality protecting the interests of both populations living there.

Security

With regard to the second point, security, the sad events since the end of September 2000 and, beyond that, the bloodshed of the past decade at holy places in Jerusalem, Hebron, Nablus, and Jericho—where the great majority of the victims have been Palestinian—have shown that the way in which both sides have exercised control over sites considered sacred by the other has been far from satisfactory. Certainly the current status quo at the holy places in Jerusalem is intolerable for the Palestinians, who have seen worshippers killed at the country's most sacred Muslim site three times in ten years: in October 1990, September 1996, and September 2000, when seventeen, three, and seven Palestinians, respectively, were killed by the gunfire of Israeli security forces in and around the Haram al-Sharif.

The establishment of a mutually acceptable regime for control over and security in the Muslim, Christian, and Jewish holy places will thus require an uninhibited and imaginative exploration of all the options. It will require as well a major de-escalation of the rhetoric on both sides. But such a de-escalation is unlikely as long as the new Israeli government under Ariel Sharon remains in office. Hopefully, the 65 percent majority of the Israeli electorate who did not vote for Sharon on 6 February 2001 will eventually express itself, and perhaps a de-escalation of rhetoric and serious consideration of this matter will be possible.

The bottom line as far as a satisfactory regime for holy places in Jerusalem is concerned involves one of two options. The first is some sort of Palestinian control over all Muslim and Christian holy places, sacred sites, and places of religious significance in both East and West Jerusalem, with matching Israeli control over similar Jewish sites on both sides of the city. These would include both the Jewish Mount of Olives Cemetery in East Jerusalem and the badly neglected historic Muslim Mamilla Cemetery in West Jerusalem. Arrangements for the security of worshippers that do not infringe on the security of local residents also would have to be worked out.

The second option is the establishment of a neutral and mutually acceptable international, or possibly interfaith, authority over all sacred sites in both East and West Jerusalem, and perhaps beyond them in the rest of Palestine/Israel. This could be either a temporary or permanent arrangement and would have to be coupled with mutually acceptable security arrangements—possibly with an international component—both for worshippers and other citizens.

Palestinian sovereignty over Jerusalem, as a unit, with contiguity of its Arab neighborhoods and with connections to its hinterland in the West Bank to the north, south, and east is essential, in part because of the serious flaws in the Jerusalem proposals that were tabled during the Palestinian-Israeli negotiations that went on from the Camp David summit in July 2000 until a week before the Israeli elections in February 2001. These proposals have been declared "off the table" after the Barak government's electoral defeat and after the end of the Clinton administration, which had served as their midwife. They will remain off the table until the new government headed by Sharon has run its hopefully brief course, since Sharon has pledged to reject any serious negotiations regarding Jerusalem. But as we have seen in the past, once a proposal has been placed on the table, it has a way of remaining there, even with the passage of time and with modifications to reflect changed conditions. Presumably, this will be the case with the Barak-Clinton proposals on Jerusalem as well.

Jerusalem Is the Key

What were the merits of these proposals, and what was wrong with them? Their primary merit was that for the first time Israel accepted that it cannot maintain control over at least some of the Arab-populated areas of occupied East Jerusalem. However, in spite of this merit, these proposals gave primacy to the security, circulation, and other needs of the Israeli population of occupied Arab East Jerusalem. The majority Palestinians were obliged to accommodate themselves to this population illegally settled by its government in occupied territory, on confiscated Arab land, in violation of the Fourth Geneva Convention, Security Council resolutions, and international law.

The result, which can be seen from maps that project the implications on the ground of the Barak-Clinton proposals, is a series of small Palestinian-controlled islands in a sea of Israeli-controlled Jerusalem stretching without interruption from the far west of the city to the Ma'ale Adumim settlement in the east. According to these proposals, Palestinian East Jerusalem would have neither the contiguity of its neighborhoods nor connections to its hinterland in the West Bank. Most of the land in the Jerusalem area would have been annexed to Israel and reserved for the use of the city's Jewish residents.

Today we are far from a substantive discussion of any of these matters, as Ariel Sharon's bellicose and expansionist declarations during his postelection visit to the Western Wall and the explosion the same day of a car bomb in West Jerusalem both underlined. This is not to suggest that this is merely a storm before the calm. On the contrary, we are likely to face an ugly period in the near future during which fatuous injunctions from certain analysts (like Robert Satloff of the pro-Israeli Washington Institute for Near East Policy) to the [George W.] Bush administration that it focus on crisis management and concentrate on more "serious" matters than Arab-Israeli peacemaking (such as Iraq) may be followed. Sadly, there will undoubtedly be plenty of crisis in Palestine/Israel for the new administration to manage.

The new Bush administration is understandably reluctant to become involved in the morass of Middle East peacemaking in which the grandiose aspirations of its predecessor sank. The Sharon government will refuse to move forward on these issues, preferring instead to prolong occupation, settlement, and direct and indirect Israeli control over the three million Palestinians of the West Bank and Gaza Strip under the transparent rubric of "further interim arrangements" bound to be unacceptable to the Palestinians.

Nonetheless, amid the confusion and the violence and deceptive spin-management of the eight months since the failed Camp David summit, there have been rays of sanity. Jerusalem (along with the issues of territory, settlements, and security) is one of the issues where the outlines of a solution could be glimpsed, even if a final agreement could not be reached before the clock ran out in February 2001. And few would question today that Jerusalem is absolutely central to any agreement to end this conflict. There is no alternative but to end it, because the more than 400 Palestinian and Israeli deaths of the last months (in a seven-to-one ratio) merely hint at how unmanageable this conflict can become if it is not ended.

Building a Wall Is the Only Option

By Shlomo Avineri

According to the author of this article, Shlomo Avineri, the peace process between the Israelis and the Palestinians is going in circles without making any progress. As the violence not only continues but also escalates, the likelihood of a peaceful coexistence diminishes. Instead, Avineri argues, the only remaining option is for the Israelis to create a physical boundary between Israel and the occupied territories until a more favorable environment for peace can be established. This boundary, which would take the form of a wall or fence patrolled by the Israel Defense Forces, would allow the political situation to cool down. Furthermore, the author hopes, it would give the Palestinians time to replace Palestinian president Yasser Arafat, who is seen as an impediment to the peace process by many Israelis. Although Avineri admits that building a wall, often referred to as unilateral disengagement, does not solve the extended conflict, he sees it as the only remaining option given the disintegration of the peace process. Subsequent to the publication of this article, Israel began construction of a fence around the West Bank. Israeli prime minister Ariel Sharon has also agreed to dismantle illegal Israeli settlements in the occupied territories as part of the Roadmap to Peace agreement. Shlomo Avineri is a professor of political science at Hebrew University in Israel and is the former director-general of Israel's Ministry of Foreign Affairs.

There is no longer any such thing as a "peace process" in the Middle East. The lofty goal of a permanent settlement between Israelis and Palestinians has been displaced by the short-term imperative of brokering a cease-fire. The future of Israeli settlements and Palestinian statehood remains in limbo as Gen. Anthony Zinni, the American envoy, mediates day-to-day squabbles over troop deployments and the arrests of Islamic militants. Massive attacks against Israeli civilians by suicide

Shlomo Avineri, "Irreconcilable Differences: The Best Solution to the Israeli-Palestinian Conflict Might Be No Solution at All," *Foreign Policy*, www.foreignpolicy.com, March 2002, pp. 78–80.

bombers and the capture of a ship smuggling arms to the Palestinian Authority have revealed that the situation is getting worse, not better.

Yet even if General Zinni were to achieve the impossible and convince the two sides to cease killing one another for a reasonable period, Israelis and Palestinians would find themselves exactly where they started: Facing one another across an abyss of irreconcilable differences. To imagine things could be put together again—as if the massive failure of earlier negotiations at Camp David and Taba, Egypt, never occurred—contradicts what both Israelis and Palestinians now think and feel.

To realize the enormity of the failure at Camp David, remember what the Labor-led government of Prime Minister Ehud Barak, with the encouragement of U.S. President Bill Clinton, was ready to offer the Palestinians between July 2000 and January 2001: acceptance of an independent Palestinian state; Israeli withdrawal from almost 97 percent of the West Bank and Gaza; dismantlement of roughly 25 Jewish settlements, which involves evacuating nearly 25,000 settlers; consolidation of the area under Palestinian control on the West Bank into a contiguous territory; the division of Jerusalem so that Arab areas would be under Palestinian control; power-sharing of the Temple Mount area; and acceptance of a limited number of Palestinian refugees who fled during Israel's War of Independence in 1948. Yet Yasir Arafat rejected Barak's proposals, and the Palestinian leader's only counteroffer called for Israel to accept the principle of the return of 3.7 million 1948 refugees, which to most Israelis implied that the Palestinians had not accepted the legitimacy of Israel. Barak ultimately resigned. In the ensuing elections, Likud leader Ariel Sharon won an unprecedented landslide, mainly due to the perception of a majority of Israelis that if Arafat rejected what Barak offered, there is nothing, except the dismantlement of Israel, that will satisfy him.

Since then, the brutal cycle of violence has further alienated both sides. It is equally utopian to imagine either that the Sharon government will offer Arafat more than Barak or that Arafat would now accept an Israeli offer that is much less generous than Barak's. The failure of Camp David is not a mere diplomatic blip: It vanquishes—at least for the foreseeable future—the hope for a historic compromise as envisaged by the 1993 Oslo accords, which were initially supported by over 70 percent of Israelis.

Those Israelis who would like to see the end of occupation and some sort of rapprochement are left with one deeply flawed option: unilateral disengagement. This alternative obviously lacks international legitimacy and certainly does not have the aura of a negotiated settlement. But under present conditions, it may be the least worst of all other options.

Such a plan would entail Israeli withdrawals from most of the West Bank and Gaza, mainly along the lines of Barak's proposals at Camp David; removal of around 30 isolated Jewish settlements, thus allowing the Palestinians contiguity of the areas under their control; resettlement of the 30,000 evacuated settlers within Israel proper; de facto recognition of an independent Palestinian state; acceptance of the status quo in Jerusalem, including Muslim control of the Temple Mount mosques and the surrounding compound; and erection of an effective line of separation between Israel and the Palestinian territories, with no Palestinian workers being able to cross into Israel (also making it much more difficult for terrorists and suicide bombers to enter the country).

The issue of Palestinian workers is perhaps the most controversial, yet Israel has responsibility for the economic welfare of the Palestinians only so long as it occupies them. In any case, a situation in which tens of thousands of underpaid, nonunionized Palestinian workers commute daily to Israel is not a recipe for economic cooperation and reconciliation. Rather, it is reminiscent of the Bantustan (black homelands) created by the apartheid-era South African government. Such an Israeli unilateral disengagement is obviously a counsel of despair, yet it is receiving widespread political support: On the left, both Barak and former Foreign Minister Shlomo Ben-Ami endorse different versions of it, as does one of the most outspoken doves of the Labor Party, Haim Ramon. On the center and right, Dan Mendor (a former Likud leader, now a Center Party member of Sharon's cabinet) likewise supports it, as does Michael Eitan, one of Likud's leading hawks in the Israeli Parliament, the Knesset. The former head of Israel's Security Service, Adm. Ami Ayalon, has founded a public movement calling for its implementation.

Unilateral disengagement does not solve the conflict, but as the historic failure at Camp David has shown, when high and unrealistic expectations fail miserably, they engender violence. Conceptually, unilateral disengagement also means a transition from attempts at conflict resolution to conflict management. Consider the example of Cyprus, which has been informally partitioned for nearly 30 years [after years of violent conflict] and where ongoing negotiations have until now led to a meaningful breakthrough. Yet no violence has occurred on either side of the Green Line [a boundary established to separate the warring factions], suggesting partition may not be the worst nonsolution in a world where solutions have eluded even the smartest diplomats for decades. Only when Arafat disappears from the scene and a less traumatized Israel elects a more moderate leader may there be a new opportunity for meaningful negotiations. In the meantime, a stabilized stand-off, which helps to minimize the violence, may by itself help bring about such a change.

Israel Will Work for Peace While Fighting Terrorism

By Ariel Sharon

In the spring of 2003, U.S. president George W. Bush unveiled his Roadmap to Peace, a plan to create a Palestinian state by the year 2005. On June 4, 2003, Bush met with Israeli prime minister Ariel Sharon and then-Palestinian prime minister Mamhoud Abbas at a summit in Jordan, where all sides agreed to the plan. The following excerpt is the text of the speech Sharon delivered at the summit. In it, he declares Israel's commitment to co-operate with the plan, most specifically by agreeing to dismantle Jewish settlements in Palestinian territories. However, he insists that while he is dedicated to peace, he is equally committed to fighting terrorism against Israel. Violence between Israelis and Palestinians has continued since this speech. In September 2003, Abbas resigned as prime minister, citing resistance to his efforts by Palestinian president Yasser Arafat. His resignation left the Roadmap process in jeopardy.

As the Prime Minister of Israel, the land which is the cradle of the Jewish people, my paramount responsibility is the security of the people of Israel and of the State of Israel.

There can be no compromise with terror and Israel, together with all free nations, will continue fighting terrorism until its final defeat.

Ultimately, permanent security requires peace and permanent peace can only be obtained through security, and there is now hope of a new opportunity for peace between Israelis and Palestinians.

Israel, like others, has lent its strong support for President Bush's vision, expressed on 24 June 2002, of two states —Israel and a Palestinian state —living side by side in peace and security.

Ariel Sharon, statement at Middle East Summit, Aqaba, Jordan, June 4, 2003.

The government and people of Israel welcome the opportunity to renew direct negotiations according to the steps of the road map as adopted by the Israeli Government to achieve this vision.

It is in Israel's interest not to govern the Palestinians but for the Palestinians to govern themselves in their own state.

A democratic Palestinian state fully at peace with Israel will promote the long-term security and well-being of Israel as a Jewish state.

There can be no peace, however, without the abandonment and elimination of terrorism, violence, and incitement.

Cooperation

We will work alongside the Palestinians and other states to fight terrorism, violence, and incitement of all kinds.

As all parties perform their obligations, we will seek to restore normal Palestinian life, improve the humanitarian situation, rebuild trust, and promote progress toward the President's vision.

We will act in a manner that respects the dignity as well as the human rights of all people.

We can also reassure our Palestinian partners that we understand the importance of territorial contiguity in the West Bank, for a viable, Palestinian state.

Israeli policy in the territories that are subject to direct negotiations with the Palestinians will reflect this fact.

We accept the principle that no unilateral actions by any party can pre-judge the outcome of our negotiations.

In regard to the unauthorised outposts, I want to reiterate that Israel is a society governed by the rule of law.

Thus, we will immediately begin to remove unauthorised outposts.

Israel seeks peace with all its Arab neighbours.

Israel is prepared to negotiate in good faith wherever there are partners.

As normal relations are established, I am confident that they will find in Israel a neighbour and a people committed to comprehensive peace and prosperity for all the peoples of the region.

Palestinians Require a Peace Among Equals

By Yasser Arafat

The following article, written by Palestinian president Yasser Arafat and pub-
lished in the New York Times *editorial section, illustrates the Palestinian Au-*
thority's stance on the ongoing peace process. Arafat reiterates that the Pales-
tinian people are open and ready to engage in a lasting peace, and he
condemns any and all violence against Israeli citizens by Palestinian ex-
tremists. He calls for the implementation of UN resolutions 242 (which calls
for the withdrawal of Israel to secure borders in exchange for peaceful rela-
tions) and 338 (which calls for a cease-fire and immediate negotiations for
a lasting peace). Ultimately, claims Arafat, the Palestinians desire an inde-
pendent state that encompasses all of the land that the Israelis occupied in
1967 and where Palestinians control their own airspace, borders, and nat-
ural resources. Furthermore, Arafat argues that any peace agreement must
address the right of Palestinian refugees to return to their homes from which
they fled in 1967. The right of return, which Israelis fear will tip the demo-
graphic scale in favor of Arab populations within Israel, has been a major
point of contention between the two peoples as well as internally within the
Palestinian community. If these issues can be addressed in such a way that
the Palestinians feel they are being dealt with as equals, then a lasting peace
can become a reality.

[S ince October 2000], Israelis and Palestinians have been locked
in a catastrophic cycle of violence, a cycle which only promises
more bloodshed and fear. The cycle has led many to conclude that
peace is impossible, a myth borne out of ignorance of the Palestinian
position. Now is the time for the Palestinians to state clearly, and for
the world to hear clearly, the Palestinian vision.

But first, let me be very clear. I condemn the attacks carried out by terrorist groups against Israeli civilians. These groups do not represent the Palestinian people or their legitimate aspirations for freedom. They are terrorist organizations, and I am determined to put an end to their activities.

The Palestinian vision of peace is an independent and viable Palestinian state on the territories occupied by Israel in 1967, living as an equal neighbor alongside Israel with peace and security for both the Israeli and Palestinian peoples. In 1988, the Palestine National Council adopted a historic resolution calling for the implementation of applicable United Nations resolutions, particularly, Resolutions 242 and 338. The Palestinians recognized Israel's right to exist on 78 percent of historical Palestine with the understanding that we would be allowed to live in freedom on the remaining 22 percent, which has been under Israeli occupation since 1967. Our commitment to that two-state solution remains unchanged, but unfortunately, also remains unreciprocated.

We seek true independence and full sovereignty: the right to control our own airspace, water resources and borders; to develop our own economy, to have normal commercial relations with our neighbors, and to travel freely. In short, we seek only what the free world now enjoys and only what Israel insists on for itself: the right to control our own destiny and to take our place among free nations.

In addition, we seek a fair and just solution to the plight of Palestinian refugees who for 54 years [since 1948] have not been permitted to return to their homes. We understand Israel's demographic concerns and understand that the right of return of Palestinian refugees, a right guaranteed under International law and United Nations Resolution 194, must be implemented in a way that takes into account such concerns. However, just as we Palestinians must be realistic with respect to Israel's demographic desires, Israelis too must be realistic in understanding that there can be no solution to the Israeli-Palestinian conflict if the legitimate rights of these innocent civilians continue to be ignored. Left unresolved, the refugee issue has the potential to undermine any permanent peace agreement between Palestinians and Israelis. How is a Palestinian refugee to understand that his or her right of return will not be honored but those of Kosovar Albanians, Afghans and East Timorese have been?

A True Peace Partner

There are those who claim that I am not a partner in peace. In response, I say Israel's peace partner is, and always has been, the Palestinian people. Peace is not a signed agreement between individuals— it is reconciliation between peoples. Two peoples cannot reconcile

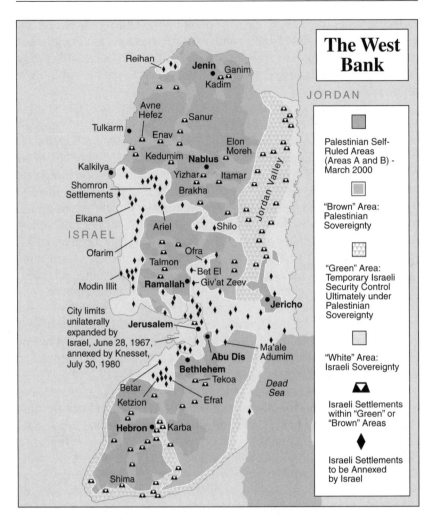

when one demands control over the other, when one refuses to treat the other as a partner in peace, when one uses the logic of power rather than the power of logic. Israel has yet to understand that it cannot have peace while denying justice. As long as the occupation of Palestinian lands continues, as long as Palestinians are denied freedom, then the path to the "peace of the brave" that I embarked upon with my late partner Yitzhak Rabin [the former Israeli prime minister] will be littered with obstacles.

The Palestinian people have been denied their freedom for far too long and are the only people in the world still living under foreign occupation. How is it possible that the entire world can tolerate this oppression, discrimination and humiliation? The 1993 Oslo Accord, signed on the White House lawn, promised the Palestinians freedom by May 1999. Instead, since 1993, the Palestinian people have endured a doubling of Israeli settlers, expansion of illegal Israeli settlements on Palestinian land and increased restrictions on freedom of movement. How do I convince my people that Israel is serious about peace while over the past decade Israel intensified the colonization of Palestinian land from which it was ostensibly negotiating a withdrawal?

But no degree of oppression and no level of desperation can ever justify the killing of innocent civilians. I condemn terrorism. I condemn the killing of innocent civilians, whether they are Israeli, American or Palestinian; whether they are killed by Palestinian extremists, Israeli settlers, or by the Israeli government. But condemnations do not stop terrorism. To stop terrorism, we must understand that terrorism is simply the symptom, not the disease.

The personal attacks on me currently in vogue may be highly effective in giving Israelis an excuse to ignore their own role in creating the current situation. But these attacks do little to move the peace process forward and, in fact, are not designed to. Many believe that Ariel Sharon, Israel's prime minister, given his opposition to every peace treaty Israel has ever signed, is fanning the flames of unrest in an effort to delay indefinitely a return to negotiations. Regrettably, he has done little to prove them wrong. Israeli government practices of settlement construction, home demolitions, political assassinations, closures and shameful silence in the face of Israeli settler violence and other daily humiliations are clearly not aimed at calming the situation.

A Peace of Equals

The Palestinians have a vision of peace: it is a peace based on the complete end of the occupation and a return to Israel's 1967 borders, the sharing of all Jerusalem as one open city and as the capital of two states, Palestine and Israel. It is a warm peace between two equals enjoying mutually beneficial economic and social cooperation. Despite the brutal repression of Palestinians over the last four decades, I believe when Israel sees Palestinians as equals, and not as a subjugated people upon whom it can impose its will, such a vision can come true. Indeed it must.

Palestinians are ready to end the conflict. We are ready to sit down now with any Israeli leader, regardless of his history, to negotiate freedom for the Palestinians, a complete end of the occupation, security for Israel and creative solutions to the plight of the refugees while respecting Israel's demographic concerns. But we will only sit down as equals, not as supplicants; as partners, not as subjects; as seekers of a just and peaceful solution, not as a defeated nation grateful for whatever scraps are thrown our way. For despite Israel's overwhelming military advantage, we possess something even greater: the power of justice.

Peace Hinges upon an Israeli Admittance of Guilt

By Edward W. Said, interviewed by Ari Shavit

This interview of Palestinian scholar Edward W. Said, conducted for Raritan *by the Israeli journalist Ari Shavit, focuses on the possibility of peace between the Israelis and Palestinians. According to Said, the conflict is unequal, with the Palestinians as the clear victims. Without a change in the Israeli mindset to allow them to see the Palestinians as a victimized people, a lasting peace cannot occur. The first step, says Said, is establishing a common narrative of events for the two peoples so that the peace process can begin on an equal footing. Edward W. Said is a professor at Columbia University in New York City and a prolific author of books and essays about the Middle East.*

A RI SHAVIT: Professor Said, this summer Israelis and Palestinians are trying to put an end to the hundred-year conflict between you and us. Can it be done? Can the conflict be resolved?

EDWARD SAID: Yes, I think it can. But I don't think Yasser Arafat can sign off on the termination of the conflict. Nor does he have the right to do so on an occasion provided by Bill Clinton at Camp David. Until the time comes when Israel assumes moral responsibility for what it has done to the Palestinian people, there can be no end to the conflict.

What is needed is a "bill of particulars" of all our claims against Israel for the original dispossession and for the occupation that began in 1967. What is needed, at the very least, is an acknowledgment of the destruction of Palestinian society, of the dispossession of the Palestinian people and the confiscation of their land. And also of the deprivation and the suffering over the last fifty-two years [since 1948], including such actions as the killing at Sabra and Chatila refugee camps [of thousands of Palestinians by Israel's Lebanese allies].

I believe that the conflict can only end when Israel assumes the burden of all that. I think an attempt should be made to say "this is what happened." This is the narrative.

ARI SHAVIT: What is the narrative? What is the conflict all about?

EDWARD SAID: It is an almost sublime conflict. I was telling [Daniel] Barenboim [the famous Israeli conductor] the other night, think of this chain of events: anti-Semitism, the need to find a Jewish homeland, [Zionist leader Theodor] Herzl's original idea, which was definitely colonialist, and then the transformation of that to the socialist ideas of the moshav and the kibbutz, then the urgency during [Nazi leader Adolf] Hitler's reign, and people like [former Israeli prime minister] Yitzhak Shamir who were really interested in cooperating with Hitler, then the genocide of the Jews in Europe and the actions against the Palestinians in Palestine of 1948.

When you think about it, when you think about Jew and Palestinian not separately, but as part of a symphony, there is something magnificently imposing about it. A very rich, also very tragic, also in many ways desperate history of extremes . . . that is yet to receive its due. So what you are faced with is a kind of sublime grandeur of a series of tragedies, of losses, of sacrifices, of pain that would take the brain of a Bach to figure out. It would require the imagination of someone like [eighteenth-century British politician] Edmund Burke to fathom. But the people dealing with this gigantic painting are "quick-fix" Clinton, Arafat, and [former Israeli prime minister Ehud] Barak, who are like a group of single-minded janitors who can only sweep around it, who can only say let's move it a bit—let's put it in the corner. That's how I see the peace process.

An Unequal Conflict

ARI SHAVIT: Is this a symmetrical conflict between two peoples who have equal rights over the land they share?

EDWARD SAID: There is no symmetry in this conflict. One would have to say that. I deeply believe that. There is a guilty side and there are victims. The Palestinians are the victims. I don't want to say that everything that happened to the Palestinians is the direct result of Israel. But the original distortion in the lives of the Palestinians was introduced by Zionist intervention, which to us—in our narrative—begins with the Balfour Declaration and events thereafter that led to the replacement of one people by another. And it is continuing to this day. This is why Israel is not a state like any other. It is not like France, because there is continuing injustice. The laws of the State of Israel perpetuate injustice.

This is a dialectical conflict. But there is no possible synthesis. In this case, I don't think it's possible to ride out the dialectical contradictions. There is no way I know to reconcile the messianic-driven and Holocaust-driven impulse of the Zionists with the Palestinian impulse to stay on the land. These are fundamentally different impulses. This is why I think the essence of the conflict is its irreconcilability.

ARI SHAVIT: Are you saying we [the Israelis] should not have come?

EDWARD SAID: Your question is too much in the realm of "what if." The actualities are too strong. To say that you shouldn't have come is to say you should leave. And I'm against that. I've said it many times. I'm totally against you leaving. The furthest I would go is to say that, given the logic of the Zionist idea, when you came, you should have understood you were coming to an inhabited land.

I would also say that there were those who thought that it was wrong to come. . . . And had I been there in 1920, I would have cautioned against it. Because the Arabs were there, and because I myself am not terribly enamoured of movements of mass immigration and conquest. So I wouldn't have encouraged it.

ARI SHAVIT: Are you willing to acknowledge that we had a need to come? That most of those who came in the twenties and thirties would have perished in Europe had they not come?

EDWARD SAID: I am one of the few Arabs who have written about the Holocaust. I've been to Buchenwald and Dachau and other death camps, and I see the connection. The chain of events. I am willing to accept that much of the evidence suggests that there was a felt need to come. But am I deeply sympathetic with those who came? Only modestly. I find it difficult to accept Zionism as Zionism. I think European Jews could have been accommodated in other countries, such as the U.S., Canada, and England. I still blame the British for allowing Jews to come to Palestine, rather than accommodating them elsewhere.

ARI SHAVIT: How about later: would you have accepted the 1947 Partition Plan?

EDWARD SAID: My instinct is to say no. It was an unfair plan based on the minority getting equal rights to those of the majority. Perhaps we shouldn't have left it there. Perhaps we should have come up with a plan of our own. But I can understand that the Partition Plan was unacceptable to the Palestinians of the time.

ARI SHAVIT: And in 1948, does the moral responsibility for the Palestinian tragedy of that year lie only with the Jews? Don't the Arabs share the blame?

EDWARD SAID: The war of 1948 was a war of dispossession. What happened that year was the destruction of Palestinian society, the replacement of that society by another, and the eviction of those who

were considered undesirable. Those who were in the way. It is difficult for me to say that all responsibility lies with one side. But the
lion's share of responsibility for depopulating towns and destroying
them definitely lies with the Jewish Zionists. Yitzhak Rabin evicted
the fifty thousand inhabitants of Ramle and Lydda, so it is difficult for
me to see anyone else as responsible for that. The Palestinians were
only responsible for being there.

ARI SHAVIT: When you look at this sequence of events, the narrative as you see it, what is your emotional reaction?

EDWARD SAID: Anger. I feel tremendous anger. I think it was so
mindless, so utterly, utterly gratuitous to say to us in so many ways,
"We're not responsible for you, just go away, leave us alone, we can
do what we want."

I think this is the folly of Zionism. Putting up these enormous walls
of denial that are part of the very fabric of Israeli life to this day. I sup-
pose that as an Israeli, you have never waited in line at a checkpoint
or at the Erez crossing. It's pretty bad. Pretty humiliating. Even for
someone as privileged as I am. There is no excuse for that. The inhuman behavior toward the other is unforgivable. So my reaction is
anger. Lots of anger. . . .

No Peace Without Justice

ARI SHAVIT: Are you saying that for Palestinians, without justice there
can be no peace?

EDWARD SAID: Yes. No one gets absolute justice, but there are steps
that must be taken, like the ones taken at the end of apartheid. Israel
and South Africa are different, but there are commonalities. They are
not entirely incomparable. One of these commonalities is that a large
part of the population feels itself denied access to resources, rights,
ownership of land, and free movement. What I learned from the case
of South Africa is that the only way to deal with a complex history of
antagonism based on ethnicity is to look at it, understand it, and then
move on. What I have in mind is something like the Truth and Reconciliation Committee. And I think we, the Palestinians, are the ones
who have to do it. Just as [South African religious leader] Desmond
Tutu and the blacks did it. Of course, they had first won. They got rid
of apartheid. . . .

But what is more important in my mind is the question of responsibility. I think it should be in the consciousness and conscience of
every Israeli that his state obliterated the Arab life of pre-1948. That
Jaffa was formerly an Arab city from which the Arabs were expelled.
And I think Israelis should be aware that their presence in many places
in the country entails the loss of a Palestinian family, the demolition

of a house, the destruction of a village. In my mind, it is your duty to find out about it. And act in consequence. . . .

Many Israelis resist this because they think the consequence would be to leave. Not at all. As I told you, I'm against that. The last thing I want to do is to perpetuate this process by which one distortion leads to another. I have a horror of that. I saw it happen too many times. I don't want to see more people leave.

ARI SHAVIT: What you are saying is that Israelis should know that, like white South Africans, they have a right to stay as long as they give up their ideology.

EDWARD SAID: Yes, an ideology that denies the rights of others.

ARI SHAVIT: So what is needed is a process of de-Zionization?

EDWARD SAID: I don't like to use words like that. Because that's obviously a signal that I'm asking the Zionists to commit hara-kiri. They can be Zionists, and they can assert their Jewish identity and their connection to the land, so long as it doesn't keep the others out so manifestly.

ARI SHAVIT: Following this logic, it would then be necessary to replace the present Israel with a New Israel, just as the New South Africa replaced the old. Unjust state mechanisms would have to be dismantled.

EDWARD SAID: Yes. Correct, let's say reformed. I am ill at ease with talk of dismantling. It is apocalyptic language. And I would like to use words that are as little as possible taken from the context of apocalypse and miraculous rebirth. This is why I don't say de-Zionize. It's like waving a red flag in front of an angry bull. I don't see what purpose it serves. So I prefer to talk about transformation. The gradual transformation of Israel. As well as the gradual opening of all Middle East countries.

ARI SHAVIT: [In January 1999] you wrote an article in the *New York Times* endorsing a one-estate solution. It seems you've come full circle—from espousing a one-secular-democratic-state solution in the '70s, to accepting the two-state solution in the '80s, back to the secular-democratic idea.

EDWARD SAID: I would not necessarily call it secular-democratic. I would call it a binational state. I want to preserve for the Palestinians and the Israeli Jews a mechanism or structure that would allow them to express their national identity. I understand that in the case of Palestine-Israel, a binational solution would have to address the differences between the two collectives.

But I don't think that partition or separation would work. The two-state solution can no longer be implemented. And given the realities of geography, demography, history, and politics, I think there is a tremendous amount to be gained from a binational state.

The Right of a Jewish State

ARI SHAVIT: Do you think the idea of a Jewish state is flawed?

EDWARD SAID: I don't find the idea of a Jewish state terribly interesting. The Jews I know—the more interesting Jews I know—are not defined by their Jewishness. I think to confine Jews to their Jewishness is problematic. Look at this problem of "Who is a Jew." Once the initial enthusiasm for statehood and aliyah [the immigration of Jews to Israel] subsides, people will find that to be Jews is not a lifelong project. It's not enough.

ARI SHAVIT: But that's an internal Jewish question. The question for you is whether the Jews are a people who have a right to a state of their own?

EDWARD SAID: If enough people think of themselves as a people and need to constitute that, I respect that. But not if it entails the destruction of another people. I cannot accept an attitude of "You shall die in order for us to rise."

ARI SHAVIT: Are you saying to Israelis that they should give up the idea of Jewish sovereignty?

EDWARD SAID: I am not asking people to give up anything. But Jewish sovereignty as an end in itself seems to me not worth the pain and the waste and the suffering it produced. If, on the other hand, one can think of Jewish sovereignty as a step toward a more generous idea of coexistence, of being-in-the-world, then yes, it's worth giving up. Not in the sense of being forced to give it up. Not in the sense of we will conquer you, as many Arabs think when they call Arafat Salah-a-Din—which means that he is going to kick you out. No, not in that sense. I don't want that dynamic. And you don't want that dynamic. The better option would be to say that sovereignty should gradually give way to something that is more open and more livable.

ARI SHAVIT: In a binational state, the Jews will quickly become a minority, like the Lebanese Christians.

EDWARD SAID: Yes, but you're going to be a minority anyway. In about ten years there will be demographic parity between Jews and Palestinians, and the process will go on. But the Jews are a minority everywhere. They are a minority in America. They can certainly be a minority in Israel.

ARI SHAVIT: Knowing the region and given the history of the conflict, do you think such a Jewish minority would be treated fairly?

EDWARD SAID: I worry about that. The history of minorities in the Middle East has not been as bad as in Europe, but I wonder what would happen. It worries me a great deal. The question of what is going to be the fate of the Jews is very difficult for me. I really don't know. It worries me.

GLOSSARY

Areas A, B, and C: The Oslo accords divided the Palestinian territories into three areas. Area A represents the area under the control of the Palestinian Authority. Area B represents the area under civil Palestinian control and Israeli security control. Area C is under complete Israeli occupation.

diaspora: People who have settled away from their ancestral home. Commonly refers to Jews living outside of Israel.

Fatah: Founded in 1959, Fatah has become the leading group within the Palestine Liberation Organization (PLO). Fatah began the armed struggle to free Palestine in 1965.

fundamentalist: A term used to describe the members of a religious community that have embraced a narrow view of their tradition. It has come to characterize people or groups who base radical political agendas on their narrow interpretation of their faith.

Green Line: The line established by the armistice following the Israel War of Independence in 1948 that separates Israel from the West Bank. In 1996 Palestinians agreed to recognize the state of Israel within the boundaries of the Green Line, allowing official Israeli control of 78 percent of historic Palestine.

Hamas: An acronym for the Islamic Resistance Movement. Born in 1987, Hamas continues the armed struggle against Israel's occupation while at the same time working on community projects for Palestinians. Hamas is concentrated in the Gaza Strip and the West Bank.

Intifada: An Arabic term for "a shaking off." Adopted as the name for the popular Palestinian uprising from 1987 through 1993. The term was reapplied to the Al-Aqsa, or second, *Intifada*, which began in 2000 and has yet to be resolved.

Islamic Jihad: A Muslim fundamentalist group that carries out terrorist attacks in the struggle to free Palestine from the Israeli occupation.

jihad: A term from the Koran, or Muslim holy text, that represents a Muslim's struggle to keep his or her faith. One aspect of this, the jihad of arms, allows for violence as a means of self-defense. Jihad is often incorrectly translated as "holy war."

Knesset: The name of the Israeli Parliament.

League of Nations: The forerunner of the United Nations. Formed by the Treaty of Versailles after World War I, the League of Nations was disbanded after it failed to prevent the start of World War II.

mandate Palestine: The borders of Palestine as they were defined when the British received an official mandate from the League of Nations to administer the territory. Mandate Palestine includes the entire city of Jerusalem and its surrounding neighborhoods.

martyr: A popular term for someone who dies while fighting for freedom and is seen as a hero by his or her people.

Palestine Liberation Organization (PLO): An organization established in 1964 by the Arab League to represent the Palestinians. The PLO became the representative of the Palestinians to the United Nations in 1974 and was recognized by Israel as the representative of the Palestinian people in 1993.

Palestine National Council (PNC): The PNC is the 669-member legislative body of the PLO, which represents Palestinians worlwide. An eighteen-member Executive Committee oversees the council.

Palestinian Authority: Also known as the Palestinian National Authority. It is responsible for directing the various government officials and organizations that were created by the Oslo Peace Accords.

Palestinian Legislative Council: The council comprises eighty-eight elected members and is responsible for internal governmental affairs within the Palestinian territories.

right of return: A term used to designate the right of all Palestinian refugees to return to their homes inside the borders of the state of

Israel. It is based on the Fourth Geneva Convention and UN Resolution 194.

settlements: A term initially used to define any new Jewish housing development in Israel. It has come to describe residential areas outside Jerusalem and within the West Bank, the Gaza Strip, and the Golan Heights. The existence and expansion of the settlements has been a source of continued disagreement.

Tanzim: The quasimilitary militia associated with Fatah. Composed of residents in the occupied territories, the Tanzim militias engage in both violent struggle against the occupation and community outreach projects.

White Paper: A government report that is used to guide policy-making decisions, such as the British 1939 MacDonald White Paper, which severely limited the immigration of Jews into Palestine.

Zionism: The political movement to resettle the Jewish Diaspora in Palestine. Zionism is now a cornerstone of some Israeli political parties.

♦ CHRONOLOGY

1907

Theodor Herzl organizes the First Zionist Congress in Basle, Switzerland, which marks the beginning of a mass Zionist movement focused on establishing a home for the Jewish people in Palestine.

1915

Sir Henry McMahon exchanges letters with Husayn ibn Ali, sharif of Mecca, promising to cede control of most of the area that would be liberated from Turkey after World War I to Arab control.

1916

The British conclude the secret Sykes Picot agreement with France, detailing a plan for the post–World War I division of Ottoman lands in the Middle East. Most of Palestine was to be left under international control.

1917

The British issue the Balfour Declaration to the Zionists on November 2, detailing the desire of the British to make a national home for the Jews in Palestine after World War I.

1922

On July 24 the British receive an official mandate from the League of Nations for control of Palestine, Transjordan, and Iraq. The French take control of Syria. The British then hand over control of Transjordan to Husayn ibn Ali, sharif of Mecca.

1936

An Arab revolt is led by Haj Amin Al-Husseini against Jews and Arabs in Palestine. More than five thousand Arabs are killed as well as several hundred Jews over three years of fighting.

1939

In response to elevated levels of violence in Palestine, the British issue the 1939 MacDonald White Paper, or policy paper, which limits Jewish immigration to Palestine to seventy-five thousand over the next five years. After five years, Jewish immigration is to end, unless the Arabs of Palestine agree to allow it. Even though the

League of Nations declares that the 1939 MacDonald White Paper is illegal, the British continue to enforce the paper's quotas through World War II.

1945
The United Nations (UN) charter is officially ratified on October 24.

1947
UN Resolution 181 is passed on November 29, calling for the partition of Palestine into two states, one Arab and one Jewish, after Britain hands over control of its mandate to the UN. In December Arab riots break out in Jerusalem.

1948
The British pull out of Palestine amid rising violence. On May 15 Israel declares its independence, which sparks the Israel War of Independence. Israel battles Arab armies from Jordan, Egypt, and Syria and eventually takes control of 76 percent of what was mandate Palestine.

1949
An armistice agreement is reached, ending the Israel War of Independence. The war leaves over seven hundred thousand Palestinian refugees. Skirmishes between Israel and neighboring Arab countries continue through the next decade and beyond.

1956
Israel invades the Sinai Peninsula, with French and British support, just months after Egyptian president Gamal Abdel Nasser nationalizes the Suez Canal. After several months, a UN peacekeeping force is deployed, and Israel withdraws.

1946
The First Arab Summit is held in Cairo from January 13 to 17, which leads to the formation of the Palestine Liberation Organization (PLO), first chaired by Ahmed Shukairy.

1967
Egyptian president Gamal Abdel Nasser closes the straits of Tiran to Israeli ships. Hostilities escalate until, on June 6, Israel attacks Egypt, destroying Egypt's air force on the ground. During the Six-Day War, Israel conquers the Sinai Peninsula, the Gaza Strip, the West Bank, and the Golan Heights as well as the entire area of

mandate Palestine. The UN passes Resolution 242 in November, calling for a normalization of relations and an Israeli withdrawal from territories it occupied during the Six-Day War. Yasser Arafat becomes the new chairman of the PLO.

1968

The PLO National Charter is adopted, and its official stance calls for the destruction of Israel.

1970

King Hussein kicks the PLO out of Jordan, an event that is commonly referred to as "Black September." PLO guerrillas then flee to Lebanon.

1972

The Israeli Olympic team is massacred in Munich by members of the Black September extremist group.

1973

On the Jewish holiday Yom Kippur, the Egyptian army retakes the Suez Canal in a surprise attack while the Syrian army retakes the Golan Heights. Israel eventually repels the Syrians and pushes all the way to Damascus in Egypt. A cease-fire is called on October 22, and Israel begins to withdraw from parts of both Sinai and the Golan Heights. The first Middle East Peace Conference convenes in Geneva and is attended by Israel, Jordan, Egypt, the United States, and the Soviet Union. Syria refuses to take part.

1974

The UN General Assembly recognizes the Palestinians' right to sovereignty, and the PLO is granted observer status at the UN.

1975

UN Resolution 3379 makes the claim that Zionism is a form of racism.

1978

The first Camp David meeting is hosted by U.S. president Jimmy Carter and is attended by Egyptian president Anwar Sadat and Israeli prime minister Menachem Begin. The meeting produces a framework for peace between Israel and Egypt and for peace in the Middle East overall. A peace treaty between Israel and Egypt is signed the following year.

1982

Israel returns the remainder of the Sinai Peninsula to Egypt on April 29. On June 3 the attempted assassination of Shlomo Argov, the Israeli ambassador to the United Kingdom, sparks heavy Israeli bombing of PLO positions in Lebanon. On June 6 Israel invades Lebanon to root out PLO guerrilla forces and surrounds the capital city of Beirut on June 13. On August 22 PLO forces leave Beirut and reestablish their headquarters in Tunis. Israel pushes into West Beirut, and on September 16 and 17 Israeli forces allow Lebanese Christian Phalange Units to enter the Palestinian refugee camps of Shabra and Shatilla. The result is a massacre of four hundred to eight hundred Palestinian civilians from the two camps.

1983

Israel begins its withdrawal from Lebanon.

1987

The first *Intifada*, or popular Palestinian uprising, begins, including both violent and nonviolent action. Money to continue the struggle comes mostly from other Arab countries and is used both to continue the fighting and to create functional Palestinian infrastructure, such as schools and utilities.

1988

Hamas is founded in January with the goal of destroying Israel. On November 15 the Palestine National Council (PNC) approves a Palestinian Declaration of Independence from its exile in Tunis.

1991

The first Gulf War starts in January. Palestinians offer support to Iraqi leader Saddam Hussein, but most of the Arab countries support the United States. Arab countries cut off a large part of the funding fueling the first *Intifada*. The Madrid Peace Conference convenes on October 30. UN Resolution 3379, which equates Zionism with racism, is repealed.

1993

Secret talks between Israelis and Palestinians in Oslo, Norway, eventually lead to the signing of the Oslo Declaration of Principles (DOP) on the lawn of the White House. The DOP calls for mutual recognition between the PLO and Israel, establishes a time line for a final peace negotiation, and allows the PLO to return to Gaza. The occupied territory is broken down into three areas: Area A un-

der Palestinian sovereignty, Area B under Palestinian civil control with Israeli military oversight, and Area C under complete Israeli control. Final status discussions are scheduled for 2000. The first *Intifada* comes to an end.

1995

Israeli prime minister Yitzhak Rabin, one of the architects of the Oslo agreement, is assassinated on November 4 by a right-wing Israeli extremist.

2000

Israel completes its withdrawal from Lebanon in May. In July Palestinian president Yasser Arafat meets with Israeli prime minister Ehud Barak and U.S. president Bill Clinton at Camp David in an attempt to complete final status talks for the Oslo peace process. A final settlement is not reached. On September 28 the second *Intifada* begins when Israeli Likud Party leader Ariel Sharon visits the Temple Mount. Peace talks begin in December in Taba, Egypt, but are unsuccessful.

2001

Ariel Sharon is elected prime minister of Israel on February 6. The World Trade Center attack by al-Qaeda operatives is carried out on September 11.

2002

Israel begins Operation Defensive Wall, barricading Arafat in his headquarters in Ramallah and pushing into the West Bank to arrest known terrorists and some Palestinian leaders. Arafat finally signs the transitional constitution of the Palestinian Authority, which guarantees basic rights but also stipulates that Palestinian legislation is to be based on the principles of Islam.

2003

Abu Mazen is elected Palestinian prime minister on April 29. The Quartet Roadmap to peace is presented to the Palestinians on the following day.

♦ FOR FURTHER RESEARCH

Books

Naseer Aruri, *Palestinian Refugees: The Right of Return.* London: Pluto, 2001.

Ebba Augustin, ed., *Palestinian Women: Identity and Experience.* Atlantic Highlands, NJ: Zed Books, 1993.

Meron Benvenisti, *Intimate Enemies: Jews and Arabs in a Shared Land.* Berkeley and Los Angeles: University of California Press, 1995.

Marwan Bishara, *Palestine/Israel: Peace or Apartheid: Prospects for Resolving the Conflict.* New York: Zed Books, 2001.

Roane Carey, ed., *The New Intifada: Resisting Israel's Apartheid.* New York: Verso, 2001.

Roane Carey and Jonathan Shainin, eds., *The Other Israel: Voices of Refusal and Dissent.* New York: New, 2002.

Muna Hamzeh, *Refugees in Our Own Land: Chronicles from a Palestinian Refugee Camp in Bethlehem.* London: Pluto, 2001.

Amira Hass, *Reporting from Ramallah: An Israeli Journalist in an Occupied Land.* Cambridge: Massachusetts Institute of Technology Press, 2003.

Theodor Herzl, *The Jew's State.* Trans. Henk Overberg. 1896. Reprint, Northvale, NJ: Jason Aronson, 1997.

Walter Laqeuer, *A History of Zionism.* New York: Holt, Rinehart & Winston, 1972.

Ian S. Lustick, *For the Land and the Lord: Jewish Fundamentalism in Israel.* New York: Council on Foreign Relations, 1988.

Shaul Mishal and Avraham Sela, *The Palestinian Hamas: Vision, Violence, and Coexistence.* New York: Columbia University Press, 2000.

Benny Morris, *Righteous Victims: A History of the Zionist-Arab Conflict, 1881–1999.* New York: Knopf, 1999.

Era Rappaport, *Letters from Tel Mond Prison: An Israeli Settler Defends His Act of Terror.* New York: Free, 1996.

Barry Rubin and Walter Laqeuer, *The Israel-Arab Reader: A Documentary History of the Middle East Conflict.* New York: Penguin, 1984.

Amnon Rubinstein, *The Zionist Dream Revisited: From Herzl to Gush Emunim and Back.* New York: Schocken Books, 1984.

Edward Said, *The End of the Peace Process: Oslo and After.* New York: Pantheon Books, 2000.

———, *The Question of Palestine.* New York: Times Books, 1979.

Tom Segev, *One Palestine, Complete: Jews and Arabs Under the British Mandate.* New York: Metropolitan Books, 2001.

Avi Shlaim, *The Iron Wall: Israel and the Arab World.* New York: W.W. Norton, 2000.

Mark Tessler, *A History of the Israeli-Palestinian Conflict.* Bloomington: Indiana University Press, 1994.

S. Ilan Troen, *Imagining Zion: Dreams, Designs, and Realities in a Century of Jewish Settlement.* New Haven, CT: Yale University Press, 2003.

Periodicals

Hussein Agha and Robert Malley, "Camp David and After: An Exchange (2. A Reply to Ehud Barak)," *New York Review of Books,* June 13, 2002.

———, "Camp David: The Tragedy of Errors," *New York Review of Books,* August 9, 2001.

Karen Armstrong, "The Holiness of Jerusalem: Asset or Burden?" *Journal of Palestine Studies,* Spring 1998.

Ida Audeh, "Narrative of Siege: Eye-Witness Testimonies from Jenin, Bethlehem, and Nablus," *Journal of Palestine Studies,* Summer 2002.

Allan C. Brownfeld, "The Growing Danger of Turning the Palestinian-Israeli Conflict into a Jewish-Muslim Religious War," *Washington Report on Middle East Affairs,* April 2001.

Helena Cobban, "Fenced In: As Arafat Declines and Israel's Grip

Tightens, the Middle East Sinks into Hopelessness," *Boston Review*, Summer 2002.

Sakr Abu Fakhr, "Voices from the Golan," *Journal of Palestine Studies*, Summer 2000.

Yossi Klein Halevi, "How Despair Is Transforming Israel: The Wall," *New Republic*, July 8, 2002.

Rema Hammami, "Interregnum: Palestine After Operation Defensive Shield," *Middle East Report*, Summer 2002.

———, "An Interview with Asmi Bishara," *Tikkun*, November/December 2001.

———, "Land and Occupation: A Legal Review," *Palestine-Israeli Journal of Politics, Economics, and Culture*, 1999.

———, "Mideast Turmoil: The President's Words of Warning: 'Things Must Change in the Middle East,'" *New York Times*, June 25, 2002.

Benny Morris, "Camp David and After: An Exchange (1. An Interview with Ehud Barak)," *New York Review of Books*, June 13, 2002.

Benny Morris and Ehud Barak, reply by Hussein Agha and Robert Malley, "Camp David and After—Continued," *New York Review of Books*, June 27, 2003.

Romesh Ratnesar, "Season of Revenge: The Inside Story of How Israel Imprisoned Arafat—and Why the Rage Keeps Burning," *Time*, April 8, 2002.

Mariam Shahin, "Violence for Violence Sake? The Roots of Terrorism Are Usually Sown and Nurtured in Climates of Deprivation and Deep Political Discontent," *Middle East*, November 2001.

Khalil Shikaki, "Palestinians Divided," *Foreign Affairs*, January/February 2002.

Saul Singer, "Paradigms for a Mideast Peace (as Time Changes Sides)," *New Leader*, March/April 2002.

Richard Swift, "The Occupation Is Killing Us All," *New Internationalist*, August 2002.

David C. Unger, "Maps of War, Maps of Peace: Finding a Two-State Solution to the Israeli-Palestinian Question," *World Policy Journal*, Summer 2002.

Graham Usher, "Facing Defeat: The Intifada Two Years On," *Journal of Palestine Studies*, Winter 2003.

Websites

Haaretz Daily, www.haaretzdaily.com. *Haaretz* is one of Israel's largest daily newspapers. Its website is updated over the course of the day and follows current events in both the occupied territories and the international community.

Israel Defense Forces Official Website, www.idf.il. This is the official website of the Israel Defense Forces, which contains up-to-date statistics on terrorist activities and casualties over the course of the second *Intifada* as well as information about the group's history and philosophy.

Israel Official Website, www.info.gov.il. This site is a good source of general cultural information about the Israelis, their government, and their country.

Jerusalem Media and Communication Center, www.jmcc.org. Founded in 1988 by a group of Palestinian journalists and researchers, the Jerusalem Media and Communications Center provides poll statistics and research reports about the Palestinian people. It also publishes the *Palestine Report*.

Middle East Research and Information Project, www.merip.org. Based in Washington, this nonprofit, nongovernmental organization publishes the quarterly print and online journal the *Middle East Report*.

Palestine Center for Human Rights, www.pchr.org. The Palestine Center for Human Rights website has up-to-date statistics on issues related to the Al-Aqsa *Intifada*. It also publishes a weekly online report regarding human rights violations in the occupied territories.

Peace Now!, www.peacenow.org. Peace Now! is an organization that was formed by Iraeli army reserve officers who believe only a negotiated settlement can bring peace. On its website, it publishes the *Middle East Peace Report*, which gives up-to-date news on peace efforts and current events in Israel.

United Nations, www.un.org. This is the official website of the United Nations, which has information relating to the current activities of the organization as well as an archive of all the resolutions relating to the Israel-Palestine conflict.